Survival Solutio

For the Economy, Biodiversity, Climate

Photo by: Miriam Kennet

Sukriti Anand and Miriam Kennet

Published by The Green Economics Institute

2021

The Green Economics Institute (GEI)

Survival Solutions: For the economy, biodiversity climate and health

Published by The Green Economics Institute www.greeneconomicsinstitute.org.uk

Registered Office: 6 Strachey Close, Tidmarsh, Reading RG8 8EP
greeneconomicsinstitute@yahoo.com

Edited by Sukriti Anand and Miriam Kennet

Printed on FSC approved stock by Marston Book Services Ltd and PrintForce.

Survival Solutions

Contents

About
The Green Economics Institute

Photo Bogusia Igielska

The Green Economics Institute has been working to create and establish a discipline or school of Economics called "Green Economics", which aims to change cultural norms and seeks to reform mainstream economics itself into a well-defined goals-based discipline which provides practical answers to existing and future problems incorporating knowledge and complex interactions into an holistic understanding of the issues. This is a diverse, interdisciplinary culture spreading very fast around the globe. We aims to prevent further runaway climate change and to stop the 6th ever mass extinction of species and to create a world of social and environmental and economic justice.

Growth and the artificially engineered High Mass Consumption which accompanies it over the last 40 years have created an over exhaustion of the planets resources and an unhealthy, unsustainable and unequal society in which 99% of people are economically disempowered. The world's economy instead of concentrating on well-being for everybody has turned into a machine to please approximately 1% of the global population and who continue to cream off the best for themselves. This creates tension and geo political instability. The rate of overconsumption has led to an epidemic of obesity and also resources plundered and air pollution completely out of control.

The Green Economics Institute brings together its students and campaigners, educators, policy makers and the public to encourage them to show each other the different perspectives and the very real choices available to them and how they can indeed choose to do things differently. It uses complexity, holism, pluralism and interdisciplinary working in order to widen the scope of economics, adding the science from the green aspects, and the social ideas from economics discourses. We seek to avoid incomplete simplistic ungrounded and partial explanations or solutions and try to establish truth and fact, helping people guard against the often biased and partial perspectives of power elites in some discourses.

The Institute has begun to influence the methodology of mainstream economics, according to Professor Tony Lawson of Cambridge University's Economics Department (2007). It uses trans-disciplinary and interdisciplinary methods so that it can factor in the complexity of nature into economics. It seeks to provide all people everywhere, non-human species, the planet and earth systems with a decent level of well-being based on practical and theoretical approaches targeting both methodology and knowledge and based a comprehensive reform of the current economic mainstream. It can, for example, comfortably incorporate glacial issues, climate change and volcanic, seismic and earth sciences into its explanations and thus in this, and many other ways, it is far more complete and reflects reality much more closely than its predecessors on which it builds.

The Green Economics Institute argues for economic development based on economic access and decision making for all. It does this by bringing together all the interested parties, who want to help, by inviting them to its events, and conferences and by means of such activities as writing books, publications and using its research, its campaigns and its lobbying and its speeches and lecturing all over the world.

The Green Economics Institute created the world's first green academic journal *International Journal of Green Economics* with publishers Inderscience. The journal is diverse and aims to be gender balanced and inclusive including voices from around the world- representing developing and developed country authors and also north, south, east and Western Europe, Africa, Asia, and other areas. BRICS, etc. It is also multi and inter disciplinary and pluralist and sits within the Heterodox School of Economics. We aim to encourage economic change and after 18 years of hard work, Green Economics now sits at the centre of the Economic Recovery and is centre stage in the mindset of millions around the world in many governments recovery programmes. Green Economic theories, policies, tools, instruments and metrics are developed to facilitate a change to the current economic models for the benefit of the widest number of people and the planet as a whole.

The Green Economics Institute carries out cutting edge research out of the box thinking in a variety of ways.

The spread of Green Economics is accelerating and hence The Green Economics Institute is pleased to bring these ideas to a broader group of readers, students, policy makers, academics and campaigners in this ground breaking volume and to begin to offer its Green Economics Solutions to help rebalance the economy and change consumerist artificial and damaging growth into growth in nature and growth in abundance and well-being of people, all species, nature and the planet.

Our official United Nations Delegations, side events and exhibition stands- at UN Climate COP Conferences presses for faster uptake of climate solutions and ambition, most recently in COP23 in Bonn, Katowice at COP24 and also COP25 in Madrid.

We have a series of more than 100 books and academic proceedings from the conferences we have run over the last 18 years. Our books provide the resources built from our research projects.

Our work is characterised by being unique and varied, diverse, and inclusive and includes people from all walks of life from all around the globe.

About the Editors

Sukriti Anand (India) is interested in issues of sustainability, ecology and the economics of energy and climate change. She has worked for almost as a consultant for a leading talent and leadership advisory in the Europe-Asia corridor, specifically focusing on the renewables and energy sector in India and Asia, tracking the growth and investments in this segment during a period of exponential growth. She holds a bachelors' degree in commerce and accounting.

Miriam Kennet (UK) is a specialist in Green Economics, she is the Co-Founder and the CEO of the Green Economics Institute. She also founded and edits the first Green Economics academic journal in the world, the *International Journal of Green Economics*, and she has been credited with creating the academic discipline of Green Economics. Green Economics has been recently described by the Bank of England as one of the most vibrant and healthy areas of economics at the moment.

Having researched at Oxford University, Oxford Brookes and South Bank University, she is a member of the Environmental Change Institute, Oxford University. She has taught, lectured and spoken at Universities and events all over Europe, from Alicante to Oxford and Bolzano, and to government officials from Montenegro and Kosovo to The UK Cabinet Office, Transport Department, National Government School and Treasury and spoken in Parliaments from Scotland to Austria and The French Senate and Estonia.She is also a regular speaker at public events of all kinds and an after dinner speaker. She has a delegation to the UNFCC COP Kyoto Climate Change Conferences and headed up a delegation to RIO + 20 Earth Summit: Greening the Economy in RIO Brazil.

She regularly speaks on TV around Europe, most recently in Belgium and Estonia and the BBC has made a special programme about her life and work. She runs regular conferences at Oxford University about Green Economics. She publishes regularly and has over 100 articles, chapters and other publications. She has been featured in the Harvard Economics Review and Wall Street Journal as a leader. Recently she was named one of 100 most powerful Unseen Global Women by the Charity One World action for her global work and won the Honour Award at the Green Business Awards from the Luxembourg Minister of Finance for her work.

List of Contributors

Liljana Popovska is a Board Member of the Green Institute, dealing with climate, corruption in environment and human rights. Member of UN Delegation at COP. Former member of the Macedonian Parliament (2002-2020), committees for environment and foreign affairs. Former Vice-President of the Parliament, Deputy Minister for development, adviser of the Mayor of Skopje, councilor in the City Council of Skopje. Worked as a researcher in the Institute of Pharmaceutical factory "Alkaloid" - Skopje. Founder and leader of the Green party DOM (2006-2018), member party of the European Green Party. Active in green public policies for environment, green economy, social justice, human rights (gender equality, disability, LGBTI, Roma), social cohesion. Active in civil sector, especially in environmental, women's and disability movements. Engineer of chemical technology, MS in technical sciences and PhD in Political Sciences (Inter-culturalism and civil society).

Adel Ben Youssef, Associate Professor at the Université Côte d'Azur, holds a PhD from The University of Nice Sophia-Antipolis. He works for University Paris Sud and EDHEC Business School before joining the University of Nice. Dr. Ben Youssef has coordinate several research projects in multi-lingual and multi-cultural setting for African Development Bank, European Commission, GIZ, UNDP, French Ministries, and Economic Research Forum Cairo. Dr. Ben Youssef has published more than 60 academic papers in different fields like (Energy Economics, Industrial Economics and Environmental Economics). His publications are in Journals like: *World Development*, Ecological Economics, *Environmental and Resources Economics, Energy Economics, Journal of Agriculture and Food Industrial Organization, Energy Policy, Energy and Development Economics, Oxford Development Studies, Technology Forecasting and Structural Change, Economic Modelling, Middle East Development Journal, Economics Bulletin, Journal of Applied Business Research, European Journal of Industrial Economics and Policy among others.* Adel Ben Youssef is negotiator at UNFCCC for the Tunisian delegation.

Dr. Mounir Dahmani is currently an Assistant Professor of Economics at the university of Gafsa in Tunisia. He earned a Ph.D. in Economics from the University of Paris-Sud in 2011 and completed post-doctoral training in Informational Economics at the Ecole Polytechnique of Paris in 2012. He was a senior negotiator for the Republic of Tunisia at COP25 summit in

Madrid. His research interests and areas of expertise include climate change, the economics of intangible assets, innovation in firms, competencies and ICTs, E-learning, Human capital and digital divides and is an author of papers in these areas. He participated in various international research projects.

Dr. Séverine Borderon-Carrez is Doctor of Environmental Law and Associate Researcher at Gredeg-CNRS in Sophia-Antipolis (interested on comparative and global law). Specialized on Global Ecological Strategy, she helped environmental engineering company in its international development, and she developed their Research & Innovation Department. She also negotiated for the Tunisian delegation in the technical negotiations on climate change at the COP24 and COP25, dealing mainly with climate finance and adaptation fund issues. As an international speaker, she was particularly invited to discuss issues of environmental diplomacy, ethical finance and climate change adaptation regarding the biodiversity loss perspectives.

Facing an increase of the number of conflicts related to resources access, environmental impact of industrial projects, biodiversity loss and climate change, her principal concern is to act quickly to preserve a sustainable and peaceful relationship between humans and nature using the appropriate methods to fluidificate communication and concerns about our internal and external environment. She recently co-founded the International Institute for Ecological Negotiation (INNÉ). The Ecological negotiation is a renewed approach to the human-nature relationship. It implies the overcoming of individual conditioning to approach humanity in the sense of the living, the common, the universal. It invites us to rethink humanity and its adaptation with regard to an inspiration drawn from Nature. The very structure of the Institute invites this opening. Since 2007, she has been an active member of several expert committees within IUCN, and she has been a member of the Climate, Natural Resources and Energy Section of the Comparative Legislation Society (SLC) since 2018.

Mike Shipley holds a degree in Zoology [External London] and in Environmental Resources [Salford.] He worked as a research assistant with the Dartington Amenity Research Trust looking at the impact of recreation on the natural environment. He gained a Postgraduate Certificate on Education from Oxford University before taking up a post at a Comprehensive school in Stockport to teach Biology and Environmental Science. He has been an active member of the Green Party since 1979, representing the Party at all levels of election. He currently convenes the

Green Party's Wildlife & Habitats Policy Working Group. He lives with his wife in the High Peak of Derbyshire.

Mariam Hussain is an independent reasercher. She is working for Research Institute of Green and Holistic Training (RIGHT) Center. She completed her Master degree from Ewha Womans University majoring in Environmental Science and Engineering. She also earned her Bachelor of Science degree from Asian University for Woman, Chittagong, Bangladesh. Her research interests include Weather Analysis and Forecasting, Tropical/ (Micro) Climatology & Meteorology, Cloud microphyscis and Parameterization schemes, Extreme weather events, Optimization and Uncertainty Quantification, Data Mining and Analysis, Machine & Deep Learning, Improvement of numerical model physics in Weather Model and Predictions for tropical regions and Bangladesh.

Nusrat Sharmin is servicing as a faculty member of the Department of Computer Science and Engineering at the University of Creative Technology Chittagong since 2018. He completed my M.Sc. in Computer Science and Engineering from Ewha Womans University, Seoul, South Korea. His current research topics are IoT, Big Data Analytics, VANET, WSN, and Machine Learning.

Dr Katherine Kennet is a child and adolescent psychiatry registrar based at the Tavistock Centre in London and an active member of the Royal College of Psychiatrists' Sustainability Committee. She has been an innovator, leader and collaborator in the field of social prescribing, devising policy and organising national events. She is currently working on the Royal College of Psychiatrists' response to the climate and ecological emergency. Dr Kennet completed her medical training at Imperial College London where she also completed an intercalated BSc degree in Medical Sciences with Global Health. She has worked in Dorset and London in the UK.

Dr Alexander Lai MRCGP MBBS BSc (Hons) is an award-winning General Practitioner (GP). He currently works at two practices in South West London and is also a resilience specialist (The Resilient Doc). His values of growth, equality and community have led to various roles supporting patients and healthcare professionals for the Royal College of General Practitioners (RCGP) and Health Education England (HEE). His focus on the importance of resilience and wellbeing is evident through his work with the RCGP Wellbeing Committee advocating for doctors across the country and as a teacher on the Lifestyle Medicine and Prevention course at Imperial College London that educates medical students on the benefits of proactive physical and mental health actions for patients as well as for themselves.

During the coronavirus pandemic he co-founded The WorkWell Doctors an organisation offering 'safe spaces' to doctors nationally to help them vocalise and manage their mental health and wellbeing issues. They've gone on to address healthcare professionals' developing needs with evidence based materials and exercises focussed around workplace wellbeing (managing stress, workload, mental and physical health factors).

Outside of work he tops up his resilience and continues to raise staff morale and promote public awareness of the plight of the NHS with the National Health Supporters Choir, a choir he helped set up during the junior doctors strikes, consisting of NHS staff and supporters, who routinely perform at rallies and conferences to support and celebrate their colleagues and raise money for mental health charities. You can find out more by following The Resilient Doc on instagram @the_resilient_doc and visiting   www.theworkwelldoctors.com

Miriam Kennet, is a specialist in Green Economics, she is the Co-Founder and is CEO of the Green Economics Institute. She also founded and edits the first Green Economics academic journal in the world, the *International Journal of Green Economics,* and she has been credited with creating the academic discipline of Green Economics. Green Economics has been recently described by the Bank of England as one of the most vibrant and healthy areas of economics at the moment. Having researched at Oxford University, Oxford Brookes and South Bank University, she is a member of Mansfield College, Oxford University and the Environmental Change Institute. She has taught, lectured and spoken at Universities and events all over Europe, from Alicante to Oxford and Bolzano, and to government officials from Montenegro and Kosovo to The UK Cabinet Office, Transport Department, National Government School and Treasury and spoken in Parliaments from Scotland to Austria and The French Senat and Estonia. She is also a regular and frequently speaks at public events of all kinds, and after dinner speaker, this week advising in the UK Parliament and the Bank of England and in Brussels on the Euro zone crisis, the high speed rail and the general economics situation. She runs regular conferences at Oxford University about Green Economics and this year has run 8 events from Youth in Action for Young People from Egypt involved in the revolution, People from FYRO Macedonia, Italy and other countries, as well as the Green Built Environment, The Greening of China as the Chinese government is very interested in her work, Women Unequal Pay and poverty, Green Economics and Methodology, truth, fact and reality with critical realism and several other events. Publishing regularly and having over 100 articles, papers and other publications, including *Green Economics: Voices of Africa, The Green Economics Reader, Handbook of Green Economics: A Practitioners Guide, The Green Built Environment, Women's Unequal Pay and Poverty, Green Economics and Climate Change, as well as a new chapter on the green built environment and climate change for Wileys publishers in Lamond, Hammond and Proverbs*. She also publishes in scientific papers, including the Latvian National Scientific Papers and Journals for example. She has been featured in the *Harvard Economics Review* and *Wall Street Journal* as a leader. Recently she was named one of 100 most powerful unseen global women by the Charity One World action for her global work.

Amber Leversedge is a master's student studying Sustainability and Environmental Management at the University of Leeds. Currently she is undertaking a masters research project about the effectiveness of environmental organisations in Tasmania developing an in-depth understanding of the complex relationship between stakeholders and the strategic nature of campaigning. She has volunteered for a variety of environmental and social organisations including the Tasmanian Wilderness Society, International Animal Rescue, and Volunteer Uganda. Amber's main interests involve visioning solutions to reduce inequality and poverty whilst maintaining ecological integrity and promoting sustainability

Introduction to Survival Solutions

This book was conceptualised on the basis of the Green Economics Institute's 15th Annual Conference titled *Survival Solutions for the Crises: Climate, Economy and Biodiversity Loss* which took place in July 2020.

The 2020 Annual Conference hosted by the Green Economics Institute revolved around the theme of Survival Solutions for the Crises and saw a wide variety of discussions take place among speakers and participants on the current crises faced by life on earth. It is increasingly necessary to view the numerous interconnected systemic social, political and ecological problems in a new light which will make us capable of addressing these issues and expand our imagination to think of new Visions for the 21st century.

The *Survival Solutions* book is divided in five parts, with each part tackling an important issue which needs urgent actions from civil society in order to build a world where everyone can thrive. These five parts tackle issues around our relationship as a society with nature, the various effects of climate change and what can be done about it, a new way of looking at economics and the economy, health and wellbeing, and corruption in non-sustainable industries which hinder transition.

This publication aims to build on the themes discussed in the conference and bring together more responses, ideas, visions and solutions from diverse perspectives to help frame the conversation around the myriad global challenges in front of us. We thank all the authors who contributed to this important book and all the readers who pick up this book, helping us to effectively further the conversations needed in order to create a better, more just world.

With *Survival Solutions*, the Green Economics Institute also aims to foster civic action and leadership, hence we encourage anyone readers of the book to transform these words to actionable paths that you can take today, however small it maybe; as several small actions can lead to big changes. The Green Economics Institute strives to combine cutting edge research with actions which increase the real world impact of the knowledge, and we encourage all our readers to do the same.

The Editors
Sukriti Anand and Miriam Kennet

Part I
Ecology and Nature

Chapter 1
Re-calibrating our relationship with Nature

Mike Shipley

This essay will explore five propositions

1. That humans arose out of nature and remain part of nature
2. Through major historical events humans have become separated from nature, starting with the separation of Earth and Spirit. These events include the Agricultural and Industrial Revolutions.
3. This separation has allowed Economics, operating theoretically outside nature to become a dominant global influence, demoting nature to a service sector for the economy
4. This sidelining of nature with the rise of capitalist economics has led to the multiple crises of today, precipitating the 6th mass extinction that will threaten human civilisation.
5. Healing the rift with nature, will help us to address these crises

The emergence of Humans

Life emerged on Earth more that 3.5 billion years ago through a process of adaptive change more complex life structures arose, with new forms building on the structure of ancestral forms. All organisms today have genes and cellular structures in common and for this reason it is postulated that all extant life shares a common ancestor, called LUCA, [Last Universal Common Ancestor.] [2]

Applying Darwin's theory of evolution by natural selection, it is possible to trace the evolution of higher life forms from early ancestors, including the hominid line that gave rise to modern humans. This line diverged from other primates some 6 million years ago with Homo sapiens emerging as a distinct species some 195,000 years ago. [3]

Our closest evolutionary relatives today are the chimps and bonobos with whom we share 96% of our genetic code. We share about 85% of our genes with mice and half of all our genes with all living plants and animals. [4] It can therefore be argued that human beings are an integral part of the whole of nature and have been molded by it.

We have no way of knowing how our early fully human ancestors regarded nature. Archeological evidence indicates that they were hunter-gatherers and to survive they would have needed an intimate knowledge of nature. Studies suggest that the earliest hunter gathers held anamistic beliefs through which they built relationships with both the living and nonliving world and that these beliefs may have reached back to our pre sapiens ancestors. [5]

The hunter-gatherer period was the longest part of the human evolutionary journey, extending back into the lives and experiences of our now extinct human ancestors and into the present day lives of some indigenous cultures. As modern human beings emerged it would be expected that they would have carried cultural and adaptive features of their immediate ancestors, and it can be supposed that would include a continuing knowledge of and close relationship with nature. This was an undifferentiated world in which humans, spirits and gods moved together within the same space, a view that still lingers in with the retention of superstitions. [6]

In citing EO Wilson's Biophilia hypothesis, which states that human beings have an "innate tendency to focus on life and lifelike processes", Eleonora Gullone [2000] notes the growing body of research that is demonstrating the relationship between human psychological wellbeing and exposure to nature. [7] She finds that there is support for the proposal that including elements of our species' ancestral lifestyle, including a close contact with nature, into our modern lifestyle may serve to enhance our psychological well-being. This suggests that modern humans do retain a psychological, as well as a biological connection with nature.

Settled Communities

As humans settled and developed agriculture around 10,000 years ago - a short time in terms of our total evolution, so our relationship with nature changed. The pantheon of ancient Sumer, taken to be the first settled civilisation some 7,000 years ago, [8] no longer worshipped the anamistic gods of the hunter gatherer ancestors but depicted gods in human form, the highest being a God in Heaven, a sky god elevated up from the base Earth.

19

This could suggest that the city dwelling Sumarians were putting themselves in a privileged position, closer to their human-like Gods than to the nature that they were conquering. [9]

Human beings had extended their range across all of Africa and Eurasia including Australia. Many different social organisations would have existed and some of the religious structures would lead on to the so called great religions of the modern world, including Judeao-Christian, Bhuddist, Confucian and Hindu. The focus here will be on the influence of Judeao-Christian, belief since this came to underpin the rise of European society and the development of the industrial capitalist economy that has come to dominate the world through globalisation and has had a most profound impact on the natural world. Other religions that are still practiced have kept some of their ancestral links with the spirits of nature.

The developing settled communities were adopting linear hierarchical structure of governance that contrasted with the more open and flexible structures of the hunger-gathers.[10]. About 4,000years ago, the so-called Abrahamic tradition of revealed truth arose in or near the Sumarian city of Ur establishing the foundation of the Judaic tradition. Early Judaism focused on one single god, but only as the most powerful, among the pantheon, not yet the only god [11]. Power to act and to command flowed from this remote god, through minor gods to the earthly priesthood and rulers to be used to control and command citizens. Power and the ability to influence outcomes no longer came from the spirits of nature.

The One God outside Nature

Human beings, with their urban hierarchies, headed by a powerful ruler identified more closely with the Divine Unseen mystery, and despite insisting that the Unseen was unknowable, nevertheless depicted the deity in human form, usually male. This established a powerful hierarchy from God to King to Subjects, with all manner of politically expedient subdivisions in between. Nature was pushed out of this relationship. The changing relationship was formalised in the early Hebrew scripts with a new mandate from the unseen God: 'to fill, subdue and rule over the Earth', [Genesis 1:28]. This mandate, eagerly adopted by the ruling hierarchies, subdued any lingering qualms that humble people may have had over the destruction of nature.

It was the Greek thinkers who developed the ideas that would lead to monism in religion and developed the view that nature's purpose was to serve human kind. Socrates expressed the view that the Gods nurtured all of life but that animals were so nurtured for the purpose of serving man [12]

The early Greek thinker Thales described a divide between the Seen and the Unseen, the Seen being the world of reality, of nature around us, that could be studied and understood. [13] This led to the development of 'scholarship' where secular information and argument was deliberately passed on from person to person, to be analysed, questioned, debated and improved. The Unseen was the spiritual world of the unknowable, the realm of the gods. Plato, then Aristotle, developed this idea aiming to close the gap between the Seen and the Unseen, the Rational world of nature and the Supernatural world of the Gods, [14]

While not referring to 'the One God', Plato spoke of a divine craftsman and Aristotle saw God as the 'Unmoved Mover'.[15]   The Greek rational thinkers observed nature and found similarities and relationships that they rationalised as an 'order' or guiding 'principle', what today we would call 'laws' of nature that operate irrespective of the interventions of gods or the interests of people. If there was a 'God' that god was represented by these principles or laws and had little to do with human affairs. This was expressed in ancient Greece as the apparent indifference of the Gods towards humans as they went about their own affairs on Mount Olympus, seemingly an early forerunner of the present day soap opera, removed from reality but nonetheless entertaining.

The idea of the two realms, the Seen world of nature and the Unseen world of the spiritual was developed by the early Christian and Islamic faiths that elevated the Unseen world described through faith above the secular world of the Seen described through enquiry and experience. [15] So contrary to the intentions of Plato and Aristotle, the gap between Secular and Divine widened and the Divine became supreme, demoting nature to the mundane world of Earthly matters.

Agricultural Revolution

One of the characteristics of human beings is our ability to alter our environment. With the hunter-gatherers this ability was moderated by the knowledge of the importance of nature and natural cycles to the supply of food and services that the tribe relied on. Hunter-gatherers today live in close harmony within their local environments. With the spread of agriculture, people came to dominate nature, they began to alter landscapes to suit their own needs and as human numbers rose, so did these impacts.

The agricultural revolution, by increasing food supply, enabled the human population to grow beyond the natural carrying capacity of the settled areas and to spread into new territories. The growing demand for food from a rising population changed landscapes and brought about extinctions particularly of mega-herbivores and carnivores that competed with humans for food. Guided by religion, human interests were accepted as supreme and our relationship with nature changed from partner to master.

Yet for much of agricultural history, farmers retained a deep knowledge of nature, understanding her ways and working with, rather than against the grain of nature. While change in nature was taking place, nevertheless the pace of change was slow.

Pre-industrial agriculture depended primarily on solar radiation as the energy source driving agricultural productivity. [16] [note that this still holds to be true, although in the industrial era agriculture has come to rely on fossil sources of primary production]. When draft animals came to be used, they needed to be fed from the products of primary plant productivity. To maintain this productivity, early farmers maintained the fertility of soil by recycling wastes both plant and animal. This can be described as eco-agriculture, agricultural practice operating within the limits and cycles of nature; it helped to preserve a high level of biodiversity. [17]

With the growth of the human population and the development of urban markets, pressure grew on farmers to produce more food. As a consequence more land was pressed into the growing of produce for market and the balance of energy flow and nutrient cycling established within the eco-agricultural system was shifted towards the production for human benefit and away from nature. Agriculture shifted from a husbanding operation to the mining of fertility.

In "The Historical Roots of Our Ecological Crisis." [18] Lynn White gives a brief review of human caused changes to the environment. White traces the emergence of man dominant over nature to early medieval period in NW Europe with the development of the heavy plough capable of cultivating the heavy clay soil - around 800AD. He notes that calendars and illustrations from that time show man clearing and ploughing, harvesting land, dominating nature. He observes that it was to be principally the descendants of these NW European peasants who would drive the industrial revolution and complete our domination of nature.

The growing industrialisation of agriculture following the industrial revolution of the late 18th to 19th Century increased the ability of agriculture to produce higher yields with the availability of artificial fertilisers, chemical pest control and mechanisation. A consequence of this was that more land was taken from a natural or semi-natural state and converted to highly managed agriculture with the consequent loss of wildlife [19]. Through specialization, mechanization, simplification and routinization, nature was bent to serve the needs of humanity. [20]

The human presumption to have a superior position over nature, reinforced by the growth of science and technology is described by Lynn Wright as: 'greatest event in human history since the invention of agriculture, and perhaps in nonhuman terrestrial history as well.' [18] The Enlightenment philosopher Rene Decarte prepared the ground for the rise of man supreme by elevating the human mind over the earthly matter of the body. To be human was to have a soul that could exist apart from the earthly realm of matter and nature. No other living thing had a soul or the ability to think and contemplate. Nature was simply a set of mechanical principles that could be understood, controlled and used. The separation of man from nature was complete, man was special, nature was a humble vassal.

Economics

With the growing power of industry and trade backed by science and technology the rise of the formal discipline of Economics as the study of the rational and beneficial allocation of resources reflected the thinking of the time. In The Wealth of Nations Adam Smith treated the Economy as a process outside nature, like a machine that conformed to rules. The market was a separate entity, guided by what Smith called the 'invisible hand', working to its own rational rules. Neither God nor nature had anything to do with it. As Margaret Schabas explains in 'The Natural Origins of Economics' economics was now detached from nature and able to produce for the benefit of man 'without limit'. [21]

Now even God was deposed from human affairs and indeed Friedrich Nietzsche declared that 'God is Dead!'. Humans reigned supreme over the Earth and the stage was set for the existential crisis of the twenty first century.

The triumvirate of rational thought, science and technology formed the bedrock of the new industrial era and it was capital that drove it. Science showed what was possible and economics provided the means to realise this. Capital was the key resource that could turn ambition into fruition. The economy changed from being about 'Oikos' - the family, their property and home, to the behaviour and flow of capital; the economy became 'Capitalist', the now globally dominant and almost unquestioned Western economic dogma that permeates all of life in the way that religion did in the medieval world.

Capital and the accumulation of money has come to dominate public and private life. Money has acquired a new function, in addition to being a unit of exchange and account and a store of value it is now the means to access power and influence. In our pursuit of money and wealth we have become blind to the intricate fabric of nature and society on which we depend.

The economy was always about human affairs, nature was nothing more than a resource, there to be exploited in pursuit of profit and personal gain. Capital became a key resource in its own right necessary to build profitable enterprises or to acquire the possessions that people needed or desired. Few people are lucky enough to be born with all the capital they are going to need in their lives, so as Yanis Varoufakis explains to his daughter in 'Talking to my Daughter about Economics' [22] most had to borrow the additional money they needed to further their life plans. This led to the accumulation of debt.

Debt was by no means the invention of the Enlightenment or Industrial Revolution; for as long as there was trade of any sort there was most likely to be debt, it seems to be a normal part of human interactions, the giving and owing of favours. But what capital debt means is that the economy, be it personal or international, needs to grow in order to repay debt, since there is a common understanding that repayment of a debt does include some acknowledgement of gratitude to the lender. In the capitalist economy this 'gratitude' is expressed as a 'fee' that means paying back more than is borrowed, this is the payment of interest. Therefore the capitalist economy requires continual growth to keep ahead of interest rates.

Human-Nature Nexus

So we arrive at a situation where human affairs, elevated to supreme status, are moderated through the actions of a human conceived economy that consumes resources taken from the natural environment that is limited in capacity by the size of the Earth. The aim of the economy is to continually grow to supply the growing demands of a growing human population and to meet the payment of interest on debt. Debt itself has become a resource that can be traded, leading to the pressure to create more debt so that it can be sold on at a profit.

Nature in itself does not have an aim, nature is the product of its own internal dynamics and relationships. One of these dynamics is towards increasing complexity and diversity for achieving such stability as is possible within an ever changing planetary environment. Nature is indifferent to human affairs even though we have a profound impact on nature. It does not - of itself, supply our needs, those who follow the Christian Western tradition, take from nature, thinking that it is their right to do so, with little thought to paying back to nature so that it can continue to produce.

Harking back to the animistic mindset of our ancestors, we easily slip into a language that portrays nature as a person, and often a generous person. We talk about nature being bountiful, of providing for us and supplying services to us. We even speak of having a 'relationship' with nature as if there was some sort of two way barginn to be struck. But nature doesn't do deals, the relationship is totally one sided. Nature will adjust to the assaults we throw at it and it is possible that these adjustments could make the planet very uncomfortable for, if not hostile to, human life. There is no law that says that nature must keep the planet habitable for human beings, that is our responsibility.

To argue that human beings are part of nature does not contradict the above assertion that our relationship with nature is one sided.. We evolved out of nature and have acquired a self awareness that has enabled us to take control of our environment. We can take knowledge of the past and apply that to the present to mould the future. We learn and apply the products of that learning to advance our own survival prospects demonstrating the advantage of conscious self awareness. Our mind is not some unknowable separate entity, our mind, like our bodies, has evolved, being selected for by natural selection, because it enhances our survival chances and that of our offspring. However, no matter how high thinking we train our mind to be, it remains firmly anchored in the body that is firmly anchored in nature. All that the body is, and all that it needs, comes from natural processes, from the air we breathe, to the food and water we consume, to the warmth and shelter we seek to the array of material comforts we need to render the mind sufficiently comfortable to have higher thoughts.

Rooted in nature we may be, but the Christian influenced Western economic society acts on the view that an advanced society sits outside the processes of nature and that human ingenuity and technology can fix any problems. To be able to mobilise our solutions to problems, it is widely accepted that we have to maintain a healthy growth economy to generate the surpluses needed to fix the problems caused by generating the surpluses. We have got stuck in a loop.

The Human Crisis

That we face an environmental crisis has been well documented. Climate is changing more quickly than we can adapt, nature is becoming depleted at such a rate that we face a mass extinction event, this one triggered by human activity. Degraded environments are damaging human health through pollution of air, water and food, the capacity of the soil to produce our food is compromised and our predation in the remaining wild habitats is leaving us exposed to an increasing range of exotic diseases. All of this is happening because we are living and operating the economy without any regard to the impact of our actions on the health of natural systems. These are crises for human beings and their society. Nature will adapt, with or without us.

Professor Partha Dasgupta observes in his interim report to the UK government on the 'Economics of Biodiversity', that economists regard the economy as operating outside the living biosphere. Any impacts are regarded as externalities and are not accounted for, so as to maximise profitability. Nature is the commons, available to all to use as they wish as a free good.

Dasgupts sets out to demonstrate to economists why it is that the economy has to operate within the capacity of the biosphere to supply, using the concept of 'natural capital'. Natural capital is defined by the World Forum of Natural Capital as : 'The world's stocks of natural assets which include geology, soil, air, water and all living things.' [23] It is from this natural capital that humans derive a wide range of services, often called ecosystem services, which make human life possible. By capitalising nature it is argued that we will come to value it and incorporate the health of the capital asset into economic planning.

But rational as it may seem in today's world dominated by economics, there are significant problems with adopting the Natural Capital approach to environmental policy, as the UK Government explicitly does in its 25 year Plan for the Environment.

Problems with Natural Capital

In reviewing some current concerns about the financialisation of Biodiversity and Conservation Sian Sullivan stated that: 'Monetising natural assets can mean that it is the money that is of value not nature itself, and that nature could be 'cashed in' to realise the money value.' [24]   Money she observes is a poor proxy for nature, the process of monetizing nature inevitably compartmentalises and simplifies an integrated complex system.

Nature is inherently unstable and variable and changes over time - it evolves. It is therefore not a good basis for building a conventional financial structure since the markets dislike uncertainty. Viewing nature like any other commodity will lead to major problems unless those involved have a deep understanding of the dynamics of natural systems.

The idea of 'bonding' nature, that is turning it into an asset to use as collateral for raising loans, and developing derivative financial instruments based on the natural asset seems to an ecologist as bizarre, but it does illustrate the present state of our relationship with nature and our 21st century value system. Value it seems can only be expressed as dollars. But nature is not a resource that can be 'sliced and diced' and offered for sale like so many chunks of beef.

Nature is not divisible, it can't be banked or cashed in. The part of nature that is identified as 'the asset' is itself part of a much larger system. That natural system may well be home to human and non-human communities, it may have intangible cultural or aesthetic value. In aiming to secure the asset and the potential gain from it, an investor might act to evict communities, stop migrations, restrict access, stop the natural evolution of the ecosystem. And what will happen to the investment and any projects dependent on the investments should the natural asset change and be perceived to have devalued before the investment has matured?

All discussions relating to natural capital and the financialisation of nature are built on the Western anthropocentric view of the world that has brought us to a point of multiple crises. The prime focus is always the interests of select groups of people. Natural systems remain as servants that supply services for the comfort of these human groups. The climate and biodiversity crises have forced themselves onto the global agenda because of the consequences for affluent society that are now starting to be felt. The crises were flagged up decades ago. Rachel Carson warned about the impending biodiversity crisis and the loss of soil fertility in Silent Spring published in 1962. The 'Limits to Growth' that warned of the problems of resource depletion appeared in 1972 the same year that the Ecologist magazine's 'A Blueprint for Survival' called for a radical change in our consumerist lifestyle that was threatening our life support system. 1972 also saw the Earth Summit and more dire warning of what would happen if we did not change our ways. But little changed and the crises gathering around us have become progressively worse and are beginning to disrupt our ways of life.

Healing the Rift

If the first four propositions of this essay are accepted: that humans arose out of nature by natural selection and that it has been the culture that we have created, including religion and economic theories, that has demoted nature to vassal status, then it is reasonable to argue that we should look to cultural change to recalibrate our relationship with nature. In this context 'culture' includes the consensus of opinion that influences our collective attitudes towards nature. It might be supposed that the growth of environmental movements over the last 30 years heralds a change in attitudes to the natural environment, however Peter Kareiva [2008] has warned of: 'Ominous trends in nature recreation' [25] citing the decline in the number of visits to national parks in America. Instead he observed that people were becoming increasingly 'videophilic' preferring to stay indoors playing video games than to go outside for recreation. This trend can lead to an 'Extinction of Experience', a term coined by Robert Pyle in 1975 [26] whereby people value nature less because they have little contact with or knowledge of nature.

Set against this trend are the findings of Natural England's 10 year report into public attitudes to nature carried out between 2009 & 2019. [27] The report finds that the number of people visiting the natural environment has increased and the length of time spent in the outdoors as progressively increased over the survey period with 65% of people questioned making such a visit at least once a week. 80% of respondents said that they 'felt close to nature' on these visits, which they found refreshing and relaxing. On attitudes to nature, 90% of respondents said that they were concerned about the destruction of nature and 62% expressed a concern for biodiversity loss. 87% reported that they had undertaken some form of pro-environmental behaviour. While the most common action was to recycle household waste, 37% reported encouraging wildlife into their garden, mostly through feeding birds.

Such surveys should be treated with some caution. Despite their findings and the high levels of membership of wildlife charities in the UK, this country was described as 'nature depleted' in the 2019 State of Nature report. [28] This report catalogues a progressive decline in wildlife since 1970. Much of this decline is attributed to the increase in the intensification of farming in a relentless drive to increase output and profit. This may be a proximal cause, coupled now with growing development pressure and the impacts of climate change, but beyond first causes there is a deeper cause, and this is our prioritisation of the health of the economy over that of nature. This is where we need to see change.

Greater engagement with the outdoors among the public, a growing awareness of the crises in nature and of climate change and the increasing engagement of young people with direct action to stop environmental destruction lays the foundations for a radical change in our collective attitude to nature. Added to this is initiative taken by Pope Francis in his encyclical Laudato Si, [29] in which he refers to our common home and the global common good, asking us to both 'listen to the cry of the Earth and of the poor.' In quoting St Francis of Assisi, he refers to 'Sister and Mother Earth who sustains and governs us'. Intentionally or not, the Pope is inviting us to reconnect with our ancestral relationship with nature as a distinct entity with which we can build a harmonious relationship, if we would but pause to listen.

This is a powerful lead by a head of state and religious leader and others need to follow, economists, financiers, legislators, politicians and the formers of opinion. To tackle to multiple crises that stem from our exploitative relationship with nature, we need to build collectively a new consensus that formally accepts what at an emotional level many of us already know, that we are an integral part of nature and that we can not continue to treat nature as a vassal to do with as we please.

Our current relationship is destructive and still built on the assumption that nature is there to serve us and that we have a right to use it as we choose. That relationship is about to end, either we will cause changes in nature that lead to an environment hostile to human civilised life, or we will learn to live equitably within the natural limits of the Earth. The choice is entirely ours.

References

2 Michael Le Page (2016) Universal ancestor of all life on Earth was only half alive, New Scientist (25.07.2016)

3 John Pickrell (2006) Timeline: Human Evolution, New Scientist

4 Chris Deziel (2018)Animals That Share Human DNA Sequences, Sciencing

5 Peoples HC, Duda P, Marlowe FW. Hunter-Gatherers and the Origins of Religion. *Hum Nat.* 2016;27(3):261-282. doi:10.1007/s12110-016-9260-0

6 Wells C, 'How did God get started' Arion, Boston University, Vol 18

7 Elanora Gullone 2000/09/01 The Biophilia Hypothesis and Life in the 21st Century: Increasing Mental Health or Increasing Pathology? Journal of Happiness Studies

8 Joshua J. Mark 2011 https://www.ancient.eu/sumer/#:~:text=It%20is%20generally%20accepted%20that,true%20city%20in%20the%20world.

9 Ancient Origins 27 April 2019 The Sumerian Seven: The Top-Ranking Gods in the Sumerian Pantheon

10 The Complex Structure of Hunter-Gatherer Social Networks Hamilton et al 2007

11 Wells C, 'How did God get started', Arion Boston University

12 Socrates, quoted in Glacken GeoJournal 26.2 103-111 © 1992 (Feb) by Kluwer Academic Publishers

13 Wells C, 'How did God get started', Arion Boston University

14 Wells C, ibid

15 Wells C, ibid

16 Guzmán, Gloria, Molina, Manuel 2009 - Preindustrial agriculture versus organic agriculture: The land cost of sustainability

17 Buck, Louise, Milder, Jeffrey, Gavin, Thomas, Mukherjee, Ishan. 2006/01/01 Understanding Ecoagriculture: A framework for measuring landscape performance

18 Lynn White 1967 The Historical Roots of our Ecological Crisis.

19 Robert 1. Papendick, Lloyd F. Elliott, and Robert B. Dahlgren 1986 Environmental consequences of modern production agriculture: How can alternative agriculture address these issues and concerns?

20 John E. Ikerd University of Missouri 1996-97 Sustaining the Profitability of Agriculture

21 Reviewed for EH.NET by Laurence S. Moss, Department of Economics, Babson College- The Natural Origins of Economics

22 Yanis Varoufakis 'Talking to my Daughter about the Economy' 2013

23 What is Natural Capital? World Forum of Natural Capital

24 Sian Sullivan 2012: Financialisation, Biodiversity Conservation and Equity: Some Currents and Concerns

25 Peter Kareiva* 2008 Ominous trends in nature recreation PNAS,

26 Pyle 1975 https://www.thenatureofcities.com/2015/03/15/extinction-of-experience-does-it-matter/#:~:text=The%20lepidopterist%20Robert%20Pyle%20first,nature%2C%20awareness%20and%20appreciation%20retreat.

27 Natural England 2019
https://assets.publishing.service.gov.uk/government/uploads/system/
uploads/attachment_data/file/828552/
Monitor_Engagement_Natural_Environment_2018_2019_v2.pdf

28 State of Nature Partnership UK 2019
 https://nbn.org.uk/wp-content/uploads/2019/09/State-of-Nature-2019-
UK-full-report.pdf

29 Laudato Si © Copyright - Libreria Editrice Vaticana
http://w2.vatican.va/content/francesco/en/encyclicals/documents/papa-
francesco_20150524_enciclica-laudato-si.html

Chapter 2

Ecological Negotiation

Séverine Borderon-Carrez

Introduction

Conventional and intensive agricultural methods allowing the work of the soil to be carried out by machines and thus reinforcing productivity are generally accepted as being responsible for the loss of biodiversity, the reduction in the nutritional value of the food they produce (thus generating health problems for the consumers), and are also accused of killing soils causing drastic loss of biodiversity. In this context, a revitalization territories and the actions of those who participate allying the human being with Nature within the agricultural process would make it possible to re-position the human in a beneficial social activity for him and his environment and to regenerate at the same time the ground, biodiversity and health of living beings in these so-called regenerative territories. To make it real, the governance of the territories needs to be reviewed and modernized through the application of new kinds of tools which aim is to reconnect humans with nature, such as the Ecological Negotiation.

Modern agriculture no longer necessarily relies on the cycles of life, nor on the rhythm of the planet. Grains and fruits grow in all seasons, regardless of the weather. Above ground, genetically modified, the productions end up on the shelves of supermarkets where consumers - little informed about the quality of the products sold - feed on industrial products from the four corners of the world and having lost all link with living things. "Today in France, it is estimated that nearly 70% of tomatoes are produced in soil-less cultivation, or hydroponics, a technological solution that optimizes space and resources, and therefore maximizes yields: plants do not grow in the ground but in porous blocks, under low-consumption LED bulbs" (Privé M, 2019).

Moreover and more generally, it is modern food that is increasingly disconnected from living things and the consequences on health are no less.

The links between food and health are widely known; nevertheless supermarkets contain these products, scientifically recognized as harmful to health, without warning that daily consumption of these products can cause serious damage to health. The ultra-processing of food reflects a strong separation between the nutrition obtained from living soils, of which the human organism recognizes the substances which it is able to ingest, digest and derive from them powerful nutritional sources, and the products industrialists transformed and disconnected from the living soils that the human body does not know how to apprehend. Without recognizable information, the organs of the human body will store information that it does not know how to process, thus generating cancer and all kinds of diseases (obstructions, obesity) due to the fact that industrial food is not natural and does not allow for the body to regenerate itself and automatically. As a result, a whole section of the population that has become intolerant of cereals, industrial milks, and processed (even ultra-processed) foods is calling for a rethink of food towards a return to so-called "living" or "natural" food. To meet this demand, it is current farming methods that need to be revisited through a return to living soils and nutritional quality through the production of food from the land.

The importance of a return to living soils

The importance of a return to living soils has been called for over several years at the international level. In this regard, the United Nations created the first World Soil Day on December 5, 2014 "in order to draw attention to the importance of a healthy soil and to advocate the sustainable management of soil resources" (WSD, 2019). The reason for this World Day is expressed in Resolution A / RES / 68/232 of 23 December 2013. The United Nations declared "that soils constitute the foundation of agricultural development, essential ecosystem functions and security food and are therefore essential for the maintenance of life on earth" whilst reminding us to be aware that "the sustainable use of soils is an essential factor in the search for solutions to the problems linked to the increase of the population and that the recognition of the importance of these resources, public awareness and support for activities to promote their sustainable management can help ensure healthy soils and thus create a world where food security and stability and sustainable use ecosystems will be assured " (UN resolution, 2013).

However, the last World Soil Day held on December 5, 2019 highlighted the evolution of land use on the planet and observation shows that current agricultural uses and practices have allowed the degradation of land by nearly 33% of the planet's soils (FAO and ITPS,2015), degradation which could reach 90% by 2050 (FAO, 2019). These degradations are, among others, due to erosion, intensive ploughing, lack of fallow land, the significant use of fertilizers / pesticides, the use of GMOs ... These agricultural techniques large-scale have a detrimental effect not only on the quality of soils, which lose fertility, but also on the nutritional quality of production, the health of farmers and, ultimately, the health of consumers. Earth and water are subject to heavy contamination that it is difficult today to stop.

For Claude and Lydia Bourguignon, both microbiologists and founders of the Independent Laboratory of Microbiological Analysis of Soils (LAMS), agriculture is today in a dead end: "Intensification has not been able to stop the famine but it has depleted millions of hectares of soil and degraded the nutritional quality of food. Based on a very reductive conception of the soil seen as an inert support, agronomy has failed to develop sustainable agriculture. Based on the successful experiences of other forms of agriculture and on the latest research in soil microbiology, Claude and Lydia Bourguignon encourage and teach all those who work the land to respect the soil as a living being and to understand its natural vocation to make it fruitful (Bourguignon, 2008). Indeed, as the French Observatory of Living Soils points out, "it is important to understand that the soil contains the greatest diversity and density of living organisms on our planet. It is a key factor in soil fertility, essential in the fight against erosion, pollution control, air and water quality. Its preservation is therefore a *sine qua non* for the sustainability of human activities and their well-being" (Observatoire Français des Sols Vivants, 2017). However, knowledge of soils is gradually disappearing. The new generations of farmers and producers no longer receive the lessons specific to the earth and the living world, to the observation of ecosystems or to agroecological tools and methods allowing of course dependence on the uncertainties of the climate whilst feeding on fruits from the soil, foods carrying genetic information capable of strengthening the health of consumers and healthy food for rural and urban populations.

Thus, in addition to the deterioration of consumer health, the consequences of this modernization of agriculture are also noticeable in terms of drastic loss of biodiversity in rural areas. The ponds have disappeared in favour of flat land, the vertiginous drop in the number of insects and birds (CESCO study, 2017) testifies to this weakening of the living world that it is urgent to revitalize, not only for reasons of ecological balance, but also for reasons of health and well-being of humanity. A return to less intensive, more varied and soil regenerating production methods such as the use of permaculture or agri-ecology are then in vogue but in a sparse manner. They require a global social consideration and a better understood land-mass integration.

Living economy, regenerative territories and ecological negotiation

An increase in demand for organic products accompanied recently by an "urban exodus" in favour of the countryside shows that a paradigm shift is underway. However, the means and tools available to meet this need for a return to nature still seem underestimated. How to give the territories the means to return to living soils? How to revitalize the activity around healthy eating? It is the whole strategy for the development of rural areas that should be reworked in order to allow a real paradigm shift integrating these new demands. In this context, the most innovative solution presented to us seems to be the integration of ecological negotiation at the heart of a process of establishing a "living economy" (Valantin, 2017) or creating 'a "regenerative territory" (Mang and Reed, 2016). These notions refer to a revitalization of the territories. The main idea is to go further in sustainable development to come up with a new design of society based on the observation and integration of humans in the natural ecosystem of life. Methodologies have been designed to implement such a new perception of land use. More precisely, for Reed, "the design process begins by attempting to understand how the systems of life work in each unique place. The role of designers and stakeholders is to create a whole system of mutually beneficial relationships. By doing so, the potential for green design moves beyond sustaining the environment to one that can regenerate its health - as well as our own » (Reed, 2007).

It is therefore a question of analyzing the resources of a territory: its strengths and weaknesses, the constitution of its population, its natural resources, its cartography, its development axes, its roads, its economic and social activities, etc. Rethink collectively a "living" restructuring of the territory. Whether it is a question of the concept of "living economy" as of "regenerative economy" or of the creation of a new "regenerative ecosystem", these so-called "regenerative" models bring the sustainability of territories to a higher level. This involves applying some principles that recognize, for example, that

> "• Co-evolution between humans and natural systems can
> only be undertaken in specific places, using approaches

that are precisely adapted; • The sustainability of a living system is directly linked to its beneficial integration into a larger system • Projects should be vectors to catalyze the cooperative enterprises needed to enable evolution • Update stakeholder systems towards a cooperative mutualism evolutive • The continued health of life systems depends on the fact that each member plays their distinctive role • A project can only create a systemic advantage in an area of benevolence, co-creativity and co-responsibility • The actualization of a self requires the simultaneous development of the systems of which it is part, etc. "(Mang et al., 2016).

For us, making use of the knowledge of territories is one point of the methodology, but then, as we can see, the deal comes up against the effective application of the methodology at the governance stage. How to make humans think as being part of an element of the largest natural ecosystem ? The establishment of ecological negotiation involves the creation of governance models specific to the qualities of the territory on the one hand and the mobilization of a new form of collective intelligence on the other.

The living economy and the regenerative territory stimulate dynamics "from the bottom up" which place the actors of the territory at the heart of the process. Like any living system, their objective is to "cooperate in diversity to guarantee creativity, efficiency and adaptability" (Valantin, 2017). Therefore, "to create a design with true durability, considerations must extend far beyond location, materials and efficiency. Designers need to look at the place, its people and the purpose - the entire living ecosystem - and continue their work from a collective perspective. The finished product must itself be an ecosystem and a sustainable economy, which are the basis of the regenerative development approach" (Mang et al., 2016).

As part of the establishment of governance specific to a regenerative territory, the ecological negotiation offers environmental negotiation (which deals with the environment), the opportunity to expand into direct dialogue with nature and the local populations affected (Borderon-Carrez, 2017). This form of negotiation is called "ecological" because it takes into account both people, their activity, their environment, biodiversity and the interactions that take place between these areas. This form of negotiation therefore obliges actors to base their decisions on a plurality of disciplines - such as natural sciences, economics, finance, politics, -, plurality of cultures (spirituality, religions) and on multi-level spatial and temporal scales. Consequently, this clarification of the stakes affects and renews the terms and procedures of negotiations (Borderon-Carrez, 2017).

In this perspective, the observation of groups of humans able to create and stabilise harmony with their environment and able to communicate with Nature as an upper level of our ecosystem of integration is fundamental. Indeed, humankind needs first to increase its level of perception to be able to acquire the knowledge of the respect of other resources, and adapt its consumption and reduce its violence to it. So as a model to go further with sustainable development and to connect humans to Nature, and following the regenerative models proposed by Reed, Mang and Valantin, we think it is necessary to have a look at the living model of indigenous tribes. Indeed, as a tool for a new vision of the territorial governance, the ecological negotiation finds its inspiration in such methodology that takes into serious consideration the potential for indigenous people to transmit deep values, essential for the survival of humankind in case of the collapse of the capitalist model. Thus, regarding anthropologic works on indigenous tribes, their ability to live outside the capitalistic world facing oppositions and with the deep-rooted desire to perpetuate their ancestral value offer them the key element to be resistant to a potential collapse of the capitalist world. Considering that, reviewing our method that to generate relations between humans and with Nature is essential as it is also essential to learn from their expertise in social innovation based on low tech. Indeed, some anthropologic studies show that indigenous tribes « increase local capacity to imagine and create sustainable alternatives. This unique phenomenon results in high social-economic innovations that offer great opportunities for learning » (Chesnais, 2019).

Ecological negotiation aims at creating a collective intelligence based on traditional knowledge and modern tools to reach a harmony humans-nature. The concept offers the actors of the territory the means to overcome the balance of power to create a real connection between the actors and with their environment. Decisions made from an ecological negotiation have as their aim to regenerate all the living elements of the territory. But to reach such a sustainable and harmonious state, at the farming level, it is necessary to switch from intensive to natural farming practices from now !

To conclude, the recreation of the Human-Nature link opens a door to a return to a shared agriculture that respects the rhythms of the planet and the cycles of life. It is therefore not only a matter of creating a dialogue between knowledge but also and above all of reworking the deep link which unites humans and living beings. The return to collective health depends on it.

Borderon-Carrez, Séverine (2017), La négociation écologique en droit des études d'impact environnemental. Droit. Université Côte d'Azur. ⟨NNT : 2017AZUR0003⟩. ⟨tel-01655020⟩

Bourguignon (2008), Le sol, la terre et les champs, Sang de la Terre, Permaculture Design.

CESCO (Centre d'Ecologie et des Sciences de la Conservation), & STOC (Suivi Temporel des Oiseaux Communs) Studies online : http://www.vigienature.fr/page/produire-des-indicateurs-partir-des-indices-des-especes-habitat

Chesnais A, (2019) https://nativeland.info/about/

Food and Agriculture Organization of the United Nations and Intergovernmental Technical Panel on Soils, Rome, Italy (2015)

Inger R. et al.(2014), Common European birds are declining rapidly while less abundant species' numbers are rising, https://doi.org/10.1111/ele.12387

Kopittke M, Soil and the intensification of agriculture for global food security, Environment International, Elsevier, Volume 132, November 2019.

Mang & Haggard (2016), Regenerative Development and Design: Evolution, in Regenerative Development: A Framework for Evolving Sustainability. DOI: 10.1002/9781119149699.ch1

Mang & Reed (2017), Update Regenerative Development and Design 2nd edition, Regenesis Institute for Regenerative Practice, Chapter 303, Encyclopedia Sustainability Science & Technology, 2nd Edition.

McBratney, et al, The value of soil's contributions to ecosystem services, in D.J. Field, C.L.S. Morgan, A.B. McBratney (Eds.), Global Soil Security, Springer International Publishing, Cham (2017)

Observatoire français des sols vivants (2016), Journal du réseau CERFRANCE, N°42.

OECD/FAOOECD-FAO Agricultural Outlook 2018–2027, OECD Publishing, Paris, France (2018)

Privé M, En Bretagne, l'agriculture intensive fait apparaître des aurores boréales artificielles, GeoMagazine, juin 2019.

Reed, Bill (2007) 'Shifting from 'sustainability' to regeneration',Building Research & Information,35:6,674 — 680 [DOI: 10.1080/09613210701475753]

Tsiafouli MA, et. al, Intensive agriculture reduces soil biodiversity across Europe, Glob. Chang. Biol., 21 (2015), pp. 973-985

UN Resolution A / RES / 68/232 of 23 December 2013, World Soil Day and International Year of Soils : https://www.un.org/en/ga/search/view_doc.asp?symbol=A/RES/68/232

Valantin.P (2017), see the website dedicated : http://www.fipan.fr/fonctionnement-du-fipan/

Wall D H et al., Soil biodiversity and human health Nature, 528 (2015).

World Soil Day, December 5th Food and Agriculture Organization of the United Nations: http://www.fao.org/world-soil-day/about-wsd/en/

Part II
Climate Change – Effects and Adaptation Strategies

Chapter 3
Climatological Analysis for Developing Agricultural Irrigation in Bangladesh

Mariam Hussain

Agriculture is one of the key sectors for Bangladesh economy significantly progressing in food availability and accessibility. Statistics show that 63% population is living in the rural areas and directly and indirectly related to agricultural works. For sustainable economic development, agricultural sector plays significant roles. However, the northern regions in Bangladesh are vulnerable to extreme weather/climate events that adversely affect the locals and country's economy. Therefore, the paper aims to asses climatology in the northern region to resolve extreme drought events by providing a mitigation tool and adaptation techniques in supporting the economy. Bogra as a representative of northern region is studied and inferred to these regions.

The climatological trend is analyzed incorporating key weather variables like rainfall (mm) and temperature obtaining data from Bangladesh Meteorological Department (1979 to 2015) and Ogimet (2016 to 2020) for 41 years for understanding drought events. The time series and regression analysis showed a positive increase in minimum temperature (for March) and rainfall temperature inferring to extreme droughts in pre-monsoon. These climatological studies are then utilized to develop a simple drought predictive model (SDPM) to mitigate droughts in the northern region by using machine learning and classification learner techniques in Matlab (2018b).

The climatological information and mitigation tool are then incorporated for utilizing in smart irrigation technology for reducing water-stress for irrigation. As northern regions still practices traditional irrigation systems and farmers utilize extensive amounts of chemical fertilizer such as urea and pesticides, these cause cultivated agro-products intake these chemicals creating pollutions in the waterbodies.

Thus, smart irrigation technology is introduced for water demands such as drip and controlled irrigation system, Moringa trees for recharging drought prone areas, and rainwater harvesting to support households and localities. The detailed climatic analysis, the SDPM mitigation tool, and smart adaptation techniques are illustrated for developing policies and contributing to regional economy as a survival solution and solidarity.

Introduction

Agriculture is a demanding sector in Bangladesh not only for growing economy but also supporting food and nutrition accessibility. After meeting the country's needs, Bangladesh also export agricultural and fisheries goods to earn foreign currencies. Bangladesh Bureau of Statistics (BBS) showed that 63% of the country's population directly and indirectly involved in agricultural works and business in the rural areas (2017). Recent global climate change is aided to more complexities and burdens Bangladesh to cope up with these challenges. Specifically, the northern regions of Bangladesh faces regular droughts and floods that significantly affect their livelihoods and eventually impact the country's development. From last decade, the frequency of such extreme events have become more uncertain and intensified so that the sufferings and losses became extremes. Fig. 1 clearly provide few examples as an evidence of droughts (left panel) and flood (right panel). By addressing existing challenges, the country is still struggling for mitigating and adapting to more vulnerable situations.

The resulting situations question to the global communities, "How does the world and global leaders justify the consequences of experiencing such extreme events in Bangladesh induced by the climate change?" One might argue stating that Bangladesh is a low-land deltaic country and pre-destined to suffer from droughts, floods, tropical cyclones, or thunderstorms. However, the question remains unanswered, "How (at what extend) is Bangladesh responsible for inducing such extreme events to be more intense?" This query leads to find a clear definition of climate variability and climate change to infer the roles of induced extreme events. First, climate variability is a natural phenomenon whereas climate change particularly temperature, pressure, and precipitation by human induced activities alter these natural processes (AMS, 2012a and 2012b, WMO, 2014). While comparing the global change, the climate interactions between largescale mechanisms to microscale environments significantly affect in the local regions.

Therefore, the interactions of global climate change and its impacts open a discussion on investigations of these local changes. The historical global climate data, period of industrial revolutions and contributions for pollutants (such carbon dioxide, methane, and toxic gases), and their impacts are well documented in the literatures. Based on these, world meteorological organization (WMO) provides some key insights for climate changes and policies (WMO, 2014). From the above facts of the global and local (Bangladesh) situations urge for providing a direction to resolve and act for the future solutions. In order to apply any solutions, there is a necessity to assess the local scenarios and specific information that will draw feedbacks for a climate justice as well as holistic resolutions. Thus, in the context of local climate change, this paper aims to address agricultural sectors and issues by assessing locally historical scenarios and extreme events that underline key solutions for mitigation and adaptation.

Background

The local changes for Bangladesh may vary according to diverse regions such as southern (mostly coastal belts and close to Bay of Bengal), eastern, western, and northern regions. However, this paper more concisely focus on northern regions because these regions represent most agricultural activities. Moreover, these regions are extremely affected by droughts and flood events that significantly hinder agricultural activities and productions. The recent studies also state that the frequency of droughts become higher in these regions (Keka et al., 2012; Al-Mamun et al., 2018; Kamruzzaman et al., 2019a; Sajen, 2020). Specifically, the prominent changes are found during the pre-monsoon season. Droughts occur when there is rainfall amount received below normal and irregular period, people may face water scarcity. According to Kamruzzaman (2019b), droughts are classified by four ways such as *meteorological droughts* i.e. delayed or below average rainfall, *hydrological droughts* i.e. no or limited surface and sub-surface water due to longer summer days, *socio-economical droughts* i.e. people and households limited access to water of daily lives and drinking purpose, and *agricultural droughts* i.e. occurred after meteorological and before hydrological droughts.

Moreover, these droughts make farmers suffer from water scarcity and agricultural sectors depend on groundwater for irrigations. These water demands increase costs and for irrigation. For instance, climatological statistics show that the northern region such as Rajshahi and Rangpur division received yearly averaged rainfall only 115 and 180 mm respectively from 1981 to 2016 (BBS, 2017). On the other, when heavy rains occur during early monsoon and monsoon, these areas suddenly experience floods. These infrequent and intensified events result in extreme water demands and extreme water availability which both impact in losses in the agricultural and economical sector. Since the rainfall and temperature directly and indirectly cause floods and droughts, agricultural productions and activities are severely dependent upon climate and/or (extreme) weather events.

The previous studies and statistical evidence show that northern regions suffer from agricultural losses and increase water demands for cultivation. The agricultural water demands require a holistic approach in resolving various environmental and sociological aspects. In order to compensate these losses, fight for climate justice, and provide feasible solutions, this paper emphasize on assessing climate scenarios, find relationship between climate/weather variables to drought events and utilize these information in providing mitigation and adaptation techniques. Eventually, for northern regions to support agricultural sectors and economy, the paper is outlined experimental methodology for section 2, climate analysis in section 3, mitigation tool in section 4, adaptation techniques in section 5, and future directions with concluding remarks in section 6.

Study Region and Experimental Methodology:

Before addressing solutions, northern regions are highlighted in the study sites. The area of interest is focused particularly Bogra city (marked in star) to represent northern regions of Bangladesh. These detailed investigations about climatological trends, regression analyses, and comparisons of historical drought events. This city is located at 22.85 °N and 89.366 °E. The city is situated nearby the Koroyotoa River connecting to major rivers like Jamuna and Brahamaputra River (shown in Fig. 1). The climate variability and/or climate change for this city is then utilized to infer scenarios for northern regions, Bangladesh. These selected municipalities and their locations are Rajshahi (24.13 °N and 89.39 °E), Isurdhi (24.133 °N and 89.05 °E), Dinajpur (25.65 °N and 88.68 °E), Rangpur (25.73 °N and 89.23 °E), and Sydpur (25.75 °N and 88.91 °E) for assessing the model performance and as well as a tool for adaptation and mitigation for agriculture. The detailed experimental methodology is explained below.

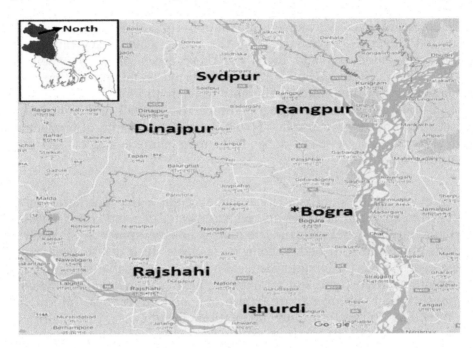

Figure 1: Northern Regions (Arrow) and the selected cities. Image (inset): Blog, 2008 and Mapdata, 2020a)

Methodology

For assessing water demands for irrigations, the daily maximum and minimum temperature (°C) and rainfall (mm) are studied. These meteorological variables are key inputs to distinguish extreme weather events such as droughts and floods (AMS, 2012a; AMS, 2012b). Furthermore, daily data are formulated as monthly averaged temperature (°C) and total rainfall (mm) for 41 years. The data is obtained from Bangladesh Meteorological Department (BMD) and Ogimet respectively for 1979 to 2015 and 2016 to 2020. The study also includes information from previous studies. Several research reported most drought events during pre-monsoon season (Keka et al., 2012; Al-Mamun et al., 2018; Kamruzzaman et al., 2019a; Kamruzzaman et al., 2019b; Afrin, Hossain, and Mamun, 2019; Prodhan et al., 2020, Sajen, 2020). Therefore, the current research incorporated pre-monsoon season (March, Apr, and May) to analyze climatological trends and to compare with drought events. Most historical drought events are obtained from Keka et al. (2012), Kamruzzaman et al. (2019b), and Afrin, Hossain, and Mamun (2019). The detailed information of data and gap-filling for any missing values are given in Table 1.

Table 1: Precipitation data and drought information

Data Types	Data availability/ Missing	Source / Gap-Filling Source
Temperature and Rainfall	1989 to 2015	BMD
Temperature and Rainfall	2016 to 2020	Ogimet
Temperature and Rainfall	2013	Ogimet
Rainfall	2019	Afrin, Hossain, and Mamun, 2019
Historical Droughts	1971 to 2004	Keka et al., 2012
Historical Droughts	1981 to 2015	Kamruzzaman et al., 2019b
Meteorological Droughts	2016 to 2019	Afrin, Hossain, and Mamun, 2019
(Agricultural) Droughts	2020	Sajen, 2020
(Modelled) Rainfall	2021 to 2025	Afrin, Hossain, and Mamun, 2019
(Calculated) Droughts	2021 to 2025	Afrin, Hossain, and Mamun, 2019

Results and Discussion

In order to find a holistic solution, the results section is outlined the discussion of climatological trend and regression analyses. These evidence are then applied to develop a drought predictive model. The model is then used to assess droughts occurrences that help can design and allocate water demands for irrigation. Finally, the results section also implement climatological event and model tool implementing improved irrigation method. Each sub-sections are described below.

Climatology and Linear regression

Since precipitation is the only input to recharge waterbodies by the natural processes, rainfall trend is the key variable for water demands in agricultural irrigations. Climatological trends for rainfall and temperature are scrutinized to find a relationship for water demands in irrigation. The time series for temperature and precipitation is shown in Fig. 2. For minimum temperature, Fig. 2c shows that March seems stronger variability about 17 to 19 °C and much lower than April and May. Though minimum temperature in March is still cooler than in April and May, the maximum temperature indicates that pre-monsoon temperature overlaps in an average range about 31 to 35 °C regardless some extreme values. Moreover, the precipitation time series is shown in Fig. 2c specifying March with lower rainfall events than April and May. It also implies rainfall in March is usually lower and quasi-stationary for Bogra district than April and May during pre-monsoon. Thus, time series analysis show more variations in precipitation and minimum temperature.

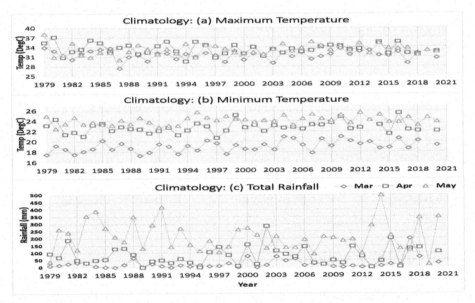

Figure 2: Climatological trend and time series (1979 to 2020) for Bogra city representing (a) minimum temperature (b) maximum temperature, and (c) total rainfall during pre-monsoon

The research also performs linear regressions for rainfall and temperature variables with time changes to attain key climatological insights. The linear dependency between rainfall and temperature might infer some historical trends. Even though, maximum temperature does not show any relationship with rainfall, the regression analysis on rainfall (response) shows a positive correlation on minimum temperature (Predictor; R^2 = 0.226) with an increasing trend during pre-monsoon (shown in Fig. 4). This implies Bogra city tends to experience rainfalls more than 23% when the daily temperature difference between minimum and maximum temperature is lower. The graph in Fig. 3 also indicates that a warmer effect in the daily minimum temperature significantly influences rainfall to increase by 23%. As Bogra city experiences droughts mostly in pre-monsoon, the increasing trend in rainfall during this season might be misleading. Consequently, it signifies to scrutinize which months are mostly affected by droughts and floods.

To clearly distinguish extreme events, each month during pre-monsoon for rainfall and temperature is tested by linear regression to distinguish droughts and floods. Fig. 3 demonstrate a significant increasing trends for minimum temperature. The minimum temperature for all months during pre-monsoon season trends are March> April> May with R^2 = 0.186 > 0.031 > 0.087 whereas the maximum temperature and precipitation have no strong linear correlations. These results imply that the increase in minimum temperature with a minor changes in maximum temperature might have enhanced water cycles by enhancing water vapor availability by evaporation and condensation processes in cloud formations. These weather variables from climatological trends by time series and linear regressions suggest that March is warmer in recent decades than the past along with lower rainfall events during pre-monsoon season. The limited rainfall in March implies to droughts whereas April and May bring torrential rains to flood the regions. When April and May do not receive rainfall or occur below normal rainfall, Bogra and nearby northern regions tend to suffer from water scarcity from meteorological to hydrological droughts.

These results also urge o clearly distinguish drought events according to Kamruzzaman et al. (2019b). Thus, there is a distinct characteristics in climate and weather events occurred from outliers which is needed to handle with special attentions.

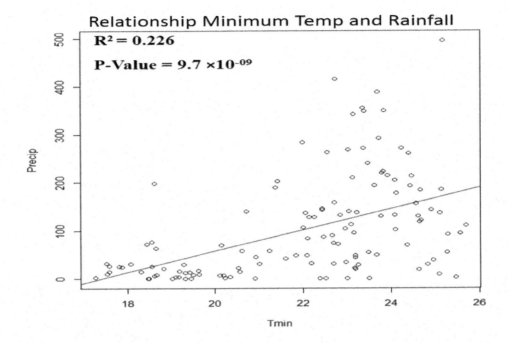

Figure 3: Positive and increasing trend between minimum temperature (°C) and rainfall (mm) during pre-monsoon for Bogra city

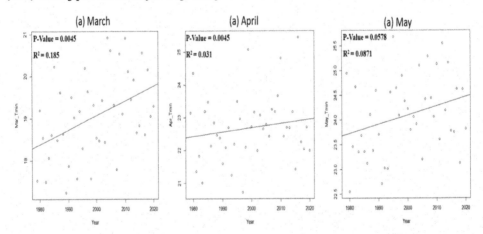

Figure 4: Increasing climatological trends for Bogra's minimum temperature in (a) March, (b) April, and (c) May during pre-monsoon season

The above results and analysis project chaotic behaviour and extreme nonlinear interactions among largescale and microscale atmospheric environment at the Bogra city in the northern regions. These results show a positive and an increasing trend between minimum temperature and rainfall observed during pre-monsoon season. As there is a positive correlation of $R^2 = 0.186$ in March with increasing climatic trend over 41 years, the climatic local condition in Bogra city infers no big changes in the region with climate (See Fig. 4a). However, the graph also conveys messages that these region is experiencing uncertain and more intensified events due to largescale climate interactions. For April and May, the rainfall and with minimum temperature show similar trend but a weaker correlation. These linear regression for climate periods in each decade illustrates that there is no or limited rainfall from winter to March with warmer temperature leading to droughts. On the other hand, April and mostly May downpour torrential rains causing floods. These results denote about uncertain interactions in resulting extreme weather events and climate phenomena which adversely affect agricultural sectors and strongly urge feasible mitigation and adaptation technology and infrastructure.

Machine Learning Algorithm

As there are historical data and events recorded in several database and presented in credible references, the art of machine learning (ML) and data science can be applied to establish a tool for mitigation of such extreme events. The simple technique in ML learns from the historical information to mimic similar scenarios via statistical and mathematical approaches. After analyzing climatology and its trends, the analysis is incorporated to test a simple drought prediction model (SDPM) in the current study. As the paper aims to provide feasible and accurate solution, the SDPM method is developed for testing its predictions for extreme drought events. Therefore, the current paper incorporate the above results, discussions, and knowledge to impose a mitigation tool for fighting droughts in the northern regions. The meteorological station provide observed data and historical events that are significant ground truth in visualizing and explaining ML SDPM. These station data provide an initial guess for interpreting any statistical or physical model results and their future projections.

Matlab is a feasible tool to model for forecasting drought events. Fig. 5 shows several simple steps to design SPDM for Bogra city. In Matlab v2018b, Classification Learner (CL) is used to categorize and forecast meteorological droughts. The details of CL assumptions and mechanisms for various classification algorithms are explained in Matlab (2020b). In

51

order to simplify the model, the drought events are expressed as two categories (1) Yes i.e. representing all types of drought events and (2) No i.e. representing no drought events. Table 1 shows all available information about rainfall data and drought events. As data pre-processing is one of key set-up for model performances, the precipitation (predictor) and drought events (response) are used in the model after analyzing the climatological trends and correlations. The Simple Drought Prediction Model (SDPM) is incorporated for precipitation and drought events for 45 years from 1979 to 2025. These data is segregated for training and validating the model respectively by 80% and 20% of the data.

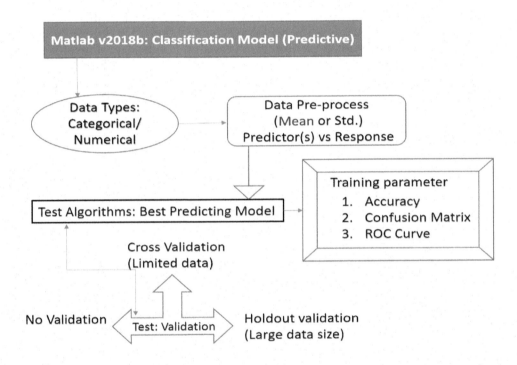

Figure 5: Developing a Simple Drought Prediction Model (SDPM) based on historical precipitation (Predictor) and drought events (Response)

While testing several CL algorithms in Matlab, the best predicting model is chosen based on accuracy, confusion matrix and Receiver Operating Characteristics (ROC) curve. The confusion matrix is created based on the true vs false prediction and positive vs negative prediction for the given data sets. ROC curve is defined sensitivity and specificity under a curve of response and predictor variables (Matlab, 2020c). The best predicting model is obtained while putting more information on training while the validation is chosen according to the size of the data. This research incorporates cross validation techniques to validate the SPDM model because of the limited observations. Allocating the given information, K nearest neighbors (NN) with weighting (option) is found most accurate model for SPDM with accuracy of 77% in limited computation time (shown in Fig. 6). In numerical modelling, computational resources and availability of true observation data are key challenges in drawing accurate and reliable conclusions. As ML is a data-driven model, the predicted results dependent strongly on the given data into the model.

Matlab Classification Models

Model	Last change	Accuracy	Features
1 ☆ Tree	Last change: Coarse Tree	Accuracy: 69.0%	3/3 features
2 ☆ Tree	Last change: Fine Tree	Accuracy: 76.1%	3/3 features
3 ☆ Linear Discriminant	Last change: Linear Discriminant	Accuracy: 64.8%	3/3 features
4 ☆ Ensemble	Last change: Boosted Trees	Accuracy: 69.7%	3/3 features
5 ☆ Tree	Last change: 'Surrogate decision splits' = 'On'	Accuracy: 74.6%	3/3 features
6 ☆ Tree	Last change: 'Split criterion' = 'Twoing rule'	Accuracy: 76.1%	3/3 features
7 ☆ KNN	Last change: Fine KNN	Accuracy: 71.8%	3/3 features
8 ☆ KNN	Last change: Weighted KNN	Accuracy: 76.8%	3/3 features
9 ☆ KNN	Last change: 'Distance metric' = 'Correlation'	Accuracy: 57.7%	3/3 features
10 ☆ KNN	Last change: 'Distance metric' = 'Cosine'	Accuracy: 65.5%	3/3 features
11 ☆ KNN	Last change: 'Distance metric' = 'Spearman'	Accuracy: 57.7%	3/3 features
12 ☆ KNN	Last change: 'Distance weight' = 'Inverse'	Accuracy: 57.7%	3/3 features

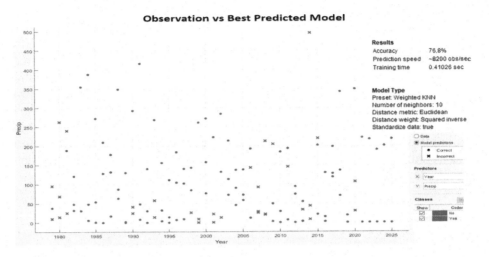

Figure 6: Tests of Matlab CL algorithms to find the best predicting model (top panel) and chosen most accurate model i.e. weighted KNN CL (bottom panel) representing performances (dots = correct) and (x = incorrect) for presence of drought (in orange color) and for absence of droughts (in blue color)

The model bias and forecasting uncertainties maybe also introduced by choosing types of mathematical assumptions in the algorithm. First, KNN is a classifying algorithm that finds relationship between [X = total rainfall] predictor (s) and [Y = drought events] response by producing distance matrix between them. The detailed information about Matlab Classification KNN is given in Matlab 2020b. These sort of algorithms may also produce sensitivities while forecasting from the model. For instance, a key sensitivity is tested for weighted KNN and shown its results in Fig. 7. One might argue stating that increasing the number of NN in the model might enhance the model prediction. However, the current paper shows that increasing NNs might increase the training period and computational resource without yielding a big difference in the forecasting accuracy. This results infer how the modelers trade of predicted results from input information, allocated computational resources, and algorithm/model sensitivities before drawing conclusions from the model. Therefore, the current SPDM is selected based on the sensitivity tests, (authentic) data availability, and computational resources for assessing the best model performance. To acknowledge the data sources for training and developing models, the performance of ML and CL models are only used cases to cases.

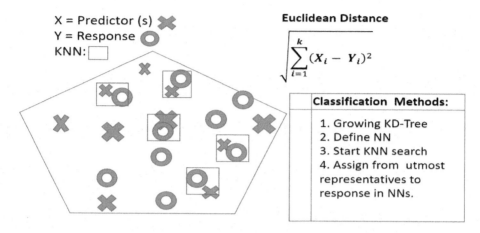

KNN Sensitivity: Number of Neighbors

Results	
Accuracy	76.8%
Prediction speed	~8200 obs/se
Training time	0.41026 sec

Results	
Accuracy	77.5%
Prediction speed	~6700 obs/sec
Training time	1.0606 sec

Model Type
Preset: Weighted KNN
Number of neighbors: 10
Distance metric: Euclidean
Distance weight: Squared inverse
Standardize data: true

Model Type
Preset: Weighted KNN
Number of neighbors: 50
Distance metric: Euclidean
Distance weight: Squared inverse
Standardize data: true

Figure 7: Mechanisms of weighted KNN algorithms (top panel) and its sensitivity for numbers of neighbors (bottom panel)

SDPM results

After training model with all available data sources and information, SPDM model is therefore is customized to predict simply droughts events with all available climatological data. The model performance is found feasible for a simple input and output relationship. The conclusions are also drawn based on the given data sets and drought information. For instance, if one inputs rainfall to the SPDM model, the model forecasts 77% accurately drought events in the month for the given region if will experience drought or not. As the SPDM is trained for Bogra city with all climatological information, the model performances are then tested applying to several other cities in the (only) northern regions. Since the northern regions have similar weather condition and climate scenarios, the model is assumed to perform well. Thus the model is applied to test its accuracy to the known information about meteorological drought events in the northern regions. Testing the model for the other cities allows drawing several key insights about model and data's predictability, reliability, and transparency.

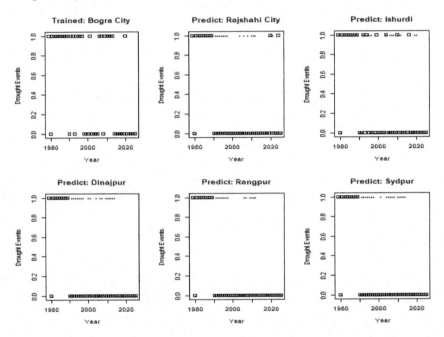

Figure 8a: Comparison observed (open square) drought events with predicted (filled dot) for March during pre-monsoon season in the selected northern regions.

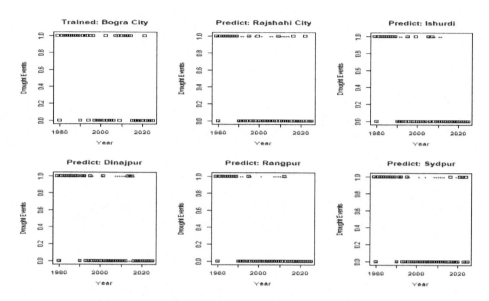

Figure 8b: Similar to Fig. 8a but valid for April during Pre-monsoon

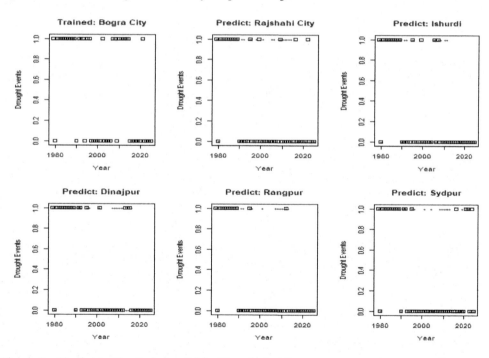

Figure 8c: Similar to Fig. 8a but valid for May during Pre-monsoon

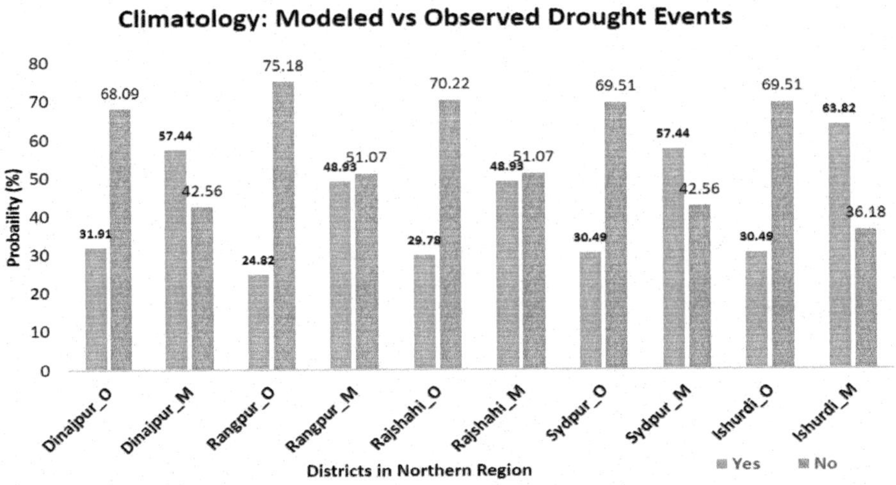

Climatology: Modeled vs Observed Drought Events

Figure 9: Tests of SPDM forecasts for selected northern regions based on data from Al-Mamun et al. (2018)

The trained SPDM has predicted drought events for northern regions such as Rajshahi, Rangpur, Dinajpur, Sydpur, and Ishurdi. First, the modeled results and its time series is given in Fig. 8 for each three months for all the cities during pre-monsoon. As the rainfall data and drought events are obtained for these region from Al-Mamun et al. (2018), the validation and accuracy of forecasts are based their data and information. This tested results suggest how the ML based CL model is dependent on data quality and availability. However, it also implies the significance of training the CL models. Since the SPDM was trained with all the aviailbe ground truth, the trained model already shows the biases according to its accuracy. For example, Fig. 9 shows a summarized prediction for each region with an accuracy for Rajshahi, Rangpur, Dinajpur, Sydpur, and Ishurdi respectively 80.85, 75.89, 74.47, 73.05, and 66.67%. In Table 2, the summary show that SPDM was trained well since the predictions have a higher range (20%) of forecasting accuracy unlike the trained model. This result suggest that SPDM model is able to capture the variations and fluctuations from the input information to output. SPDM model did not show extreme biases to the fed-data because of diverse sources and accurate information during training period. Therefore, SPDM has quite advanced forecasting predictability with reliable accuracy to be used as a mitigation tool for drought cases.

Table 2: Model performance for drought prediction in the northern region

Region (*B)	Trained	Dinajpur	Rangpur	Rajshahi	Sydpur	Ishurdi
RMSE (%)	23.2	25.53	24.11	19.15	26.95	33.33
Accuracy (%)	76.8	74.47	75.89	80.85	73.05	66.67

Application to Agricultural Irrigation Sectors:

Along with climatological analysis and mitigation tools, there is also a strong necessity for developing adaptation capacity in order to cope up with the extreme events like droughts. The paper emphasizes on adaptation capacities by several ways such as shifting traditional irrigations to controlled systems, local participations in water saving technology, and growing drought tolerant plants. As drought periods are prominent in March and April in the norther regions, irrigation water demands significantly higher. However, the northern regions practice traditional irrigation system till date which wastes water because of the uncontrolled irrigation system. Fig. 10 shows a few snapshots of traditional irrigation system around sub-districts (upzila) in Bogra city. Though fish production and agricultural lands sub-merge significantly during floods, traditional irrigation system also hampers the environment, waterbodies, and the sub-surface aquifers i.e. groundwater infiltration by leaching fertilizer and pesticides and making an eutrophication (Reddy, 2015; Sela, 2020). Therefore based on needs, piped irrigation, center pivot, or furrow irrigation system can help reducing the water-loss and save the environment and groundwater. Therefore, based on the drought events predicted by the SPDM, water-stress can be significantly reduce by incorporating drip and controlled irrigation system. This smart irrigation can also be monitored and maintained using pipelines.

Figure 10: Traditional cultivation and irrigation system in the northern regions: representing nearby areas at Sherpur and Dhnut in Bogra. (Photo: Sumayea shared 29 Aug 2020)

Besides a mitigation tool, the adaption by enhancing local participation in fighting droughts also might help in decelerating the adverse impacts of climate induced droughts. By knowing advanced warning for drought events, the drought prone localities such as Bogra, Rajshahi or Rangpur where people have lack of access to drinking water can enhance a storage to save rainwater. This rainwater harvesting is a simple engineering at their houses with a pipeline and a water tank. The harvested water is not only used for household works and laundry factories but also filtered for drinking water purposes. Moringa leaves can function as an effective filter for toxic metals or microscopic materials (Abdull Razis, Ibrahim and Kntayya, 2014; UNB, 2020d). This paper suggests utilizing Moringa leaves for filtering processes i.e. manufacturing feasible filter in the rainwater harvesting system. Moreover, a simple pipeline and a water tank can be easily placed for collecting rainwater that can easily be used for washing clothes and for households works harvest the processes forecasts about the drought events, information for also suggests drought tolerant technologies in the northern regions.

The climatological analysis and trends are also helpful to customize adaptation techniques to support the environment as well as a source of small business. As the agricultural sectors in the northern regions experience droughts in dry period, Moringa trees can be cultivated as a drought tolerant plant to support nutrition and food to households as well as small business. There are several households in Bogra cities are found growing Moringa at their backyards shown in fig. 12. These practices in local communities also help producing short income sources as well as supporting their food and nutritional values. Moreover, every possible household, highways, and big roads and its sidewalks can easily grow Moringa trees. In this way, these plants not only help drought prone areas recharging water level for the sub-surface and ground level but also help produce a source of incomes. As this plant is easily grown i.e. stems and branches can also grow itself to become trees, the health benefits of the plants also are also a good source exporting business as well (Parrotta, 2009; Abdull Razis, Ibrahim and Kntayya, 2014). Eventually, applying climate knowledge to combine the mitigation tool with the adaptation techniques is important practices in surviving and saving us from extreme events and losses.

Photo: Bubli in Bogra Sadar on 20 Aug 2017

Photo: Bubli in Bogra Sadar

Figure 12: Local Behavioral changes for adaptation to droughts using existing resources (Photo Tanjila in Bogra Sadar)

Conclusion and future direction

The local climatological analyses show several key understandings to apply these information to approach to irrigation and water demands' solutions in fighting against climate induced droughts for the northern regions. The local climatic evidence also prove that there are quite negligible contributions and changes that induce occurrences extreme events. However, these results and analysis suggest distinguishing largescale circulations interacting with microscale to intensified extreme climate/weather events by climate change. For instance, the trend analysis displayed an increase in the minimum recorded temperature with a positive relationship with rainfall events inferring key parameters to cause droughts or floods. The trend analysis also provide signals how extreme weather events are so irregular and highly chaotic. Moreover, this climatological studies provide valuable information to develop a simple extreme events i.e. droughts predictive model that can help mitigating droughts as well as agricultural water sectors. These paper also argued about the robustness of data-driven model and its transparency to utilize in the mitigation tool. The reliability for such classified model also strongly dependent upon the quality and source of the information. As the machine learning models are developed case to case basis, the limitations of Simple

Drought Predictive Model (SPDM) maybe overcome by re-training to make more general model to forecast droughts for various regions in Bangladesh. Therefore, the future directions of the paper include to enhance SPDM strengths by incorporating uncertainty quantification to correct model biases, and to model using numerically modelled weather data and events.

References

Abdull Razis, A.F., Ibrahim, M.D. and Kntayya, S.B. (2014). Health Benefits of Moringa oleifera. *Asian Pacific Journal of Cancer Prevention*, [online] 15(20), pp.8571–8576. Available at: https://miracletrees.org/moringa-doc/health-benefits-moringa-oleifera.pdf [Accessed 29 Oct. 2019].

Afrin, R., Hossain, F. and Mamun, S. (2019). Analysis of Drought in the Northern Region of Bangladesh Using Standardized Precipitation Index (SPI). *Journal of Environmental Science and Natural Resources*, 11(1–2), pp.199–216.

Al-Mamun, A., Rahman, Md.N.F., Aziz, Md.A., Qayum, Md.A., Hossain, Md.I., Islam Nihad, S.A. and Kabir, Md.S. (2018). Identification of Meteorological Drought Prone Area in Bangladesh using Standardized Precipitation Index. *Journal of Earth Science and Climate Change*, 3(3).

AMS (2012a). *Climate Variability*. [Online] Glossary of Meteorology. Available at: http://glossary.ametsoc.org/wiki/Climate_variability [Accessed 25 Sep. 2020].

AMS (2012b). *Meteorology Glossary*. [Online] Glossary of Meteorology. Available at: http://glossary.ametsoc.org/wiki/Climate_change [Accessed 25 Sep. 2020].

BBS (2017). *Bangladesh Statistics*. [Online] *Bangladesh Bureau of Statistics*. Bangladesh. Available at: http://www.bbs.gov.bd/ [Accessed 28 Sep. 2018].

Blog, G. (2008). *Welcome Bangladesh: Rajshahi Division*. [Online] GreenbdInfo. Available at:

http://greenbdinfo.blogspot.com/2008/06/rajshahi-division.html [Accessed 22 Sep. 2020].

Elgert, L., Austin, P. and Picchione, K. (2015). Improving water security through rainwater harvesting: a case from Guatemala and the potential for expanding coverage. *International Journal of Water Resources Development*, 32(5), pp.765–780.

Hoque, M.Z. and Mollah, M.A.-M. (2019). Extreme events to get more extreme. *The Daily Star*. [Online] 20 Feb. Available at: https://www.thedailystar.net/backpage/news/drought-hits-northern-areas-1959289 [Accessed 22 Sep. 2020].

Islam, Md.S. (2010). Droughts. *The Daily Star*. [Online] 23 Apr. Available at: https://www.thedailystar.net/news-detail-135551 [Accessed 22 Sep. 2020].

Islam, Md.S., Hossain, Md.Z. and Sikder, Md.B. (2019). Drought adaptation measures and their effectiveness at Barind Tract in northwest Bangladesh: a perception study. *Natural Hazards*, 97(3), pp.1253–1276.

Kamruzzaman, Jang, Cho and Hwang (2019a). Future Changes in Precipitation and Drought Characteristics over Bangladesh under CMIP5 Climatological Projections. *Water*, 11(11), p.2219.

Kamruzzaman, M., Hwang, S., Cho, J., Jang, M.-W. and Jeong, H. (2019b). Evaluating the Spatiotemporal Characteristics of Agricultural Drought in Bangladesh Using Eective Drought Index. *Water*, 11(2437), pp.1–22.

Keka, A.I., Matin, I., Rahman, M. and Banu, D. (2012). Analysis of Drought in Eastern Part of Bangladesh. *Daffodil International University Journal of Science and Technology*, 7(1), pp.20–27.

Mapdata (2020a). *Bangladesh*. [Online] Bangladesh. Available at: https://www.google.com/maps/place/Bangladesh/@23.4905831 [Accessed 22 Sep. 2020].

Matlab (2020b). *ROC Curve*. [Online] www.mathworks.com. Available at:

https://www.mathworks.com/matlabcentral/fileexchange/52442-roc-curve [Accessed 18 Sep. 2020].

Matlab (2020c). *Train models to classify data using supervised machine learning - MATLAB*. [Online] www.mathworks.com. Available at: https://www.mathworks.com/help/stats/classificationlearner-app.html [Accessed 18 Sep. 2020].

Mukherjee, B. and Adhikary, S. (2019). Water Efficient Rice Cultivation: Technological Interventions. In: A.K. Rawat and U.K. Tripathi, eds., *Advances in Agronomy*. New Delhi: AkiNik Publications, pp.35–54.

Parrotta, J.A. (2009). Moringa oleifera. In: *Enzyklopädie der Holzgewächse, Handbuch und Atlas der Dendrologie*. KGaA, Weinheim: WILEY-VCH Verlag GmbH & Co, pp.1–9.

Parvez, S. (2009). *Govt plans for drought-tolerant rice*. [Online] The Daily Star. Available at: https://www.thedailystar.net/news-detail-102846 [Accessed 26 Sep. 2020].

Prodhan, F.A., Zhang, J., Bai, Y., Pangali Sharma, T.P. and Koju, U.A. (2020). Monitoring of Drought Condition and Risk in Bangladesh Combined Data from Satellite and Ground Meteorological Observations. *IEEE Access*, 8, pp.93264–93282.

Rafiuddin, M., Dash, B.K., Khanam, F. and Islam, M.N. (2011). Diagnosis of Drought in Bangladesh using Standardized Precipitation Index. In: *IPCBEE*. 2011 International Conference on Environment Science and Engineering. Singapore: IACSIT Press, pp.184–187.

Reddy, J. (2015). *Drip Irrigation Vs Sprinkler Irrigation Farming*. [Online] Agri Farming. Available at: https://www.agrifarming.in/drip-irrigation-vs-sprinkler [Accessed 27 Sep. 2020].

Sajen, S. (2020). *Drought hits northern areas*. [Online] The Daily Star. Available at: https://www.thedailystar.net/backpage/news/drought-hits-northern-areas-1959289 [Accessed 22 Sep. 2020].

Sela, G. (2020). *Principles of Irrigation System Design*. [Online] https://cropaia.com/blog/irrigation-system-design/. Available at: https://cropaia.com/blog/irrigation-system-design/ [Accessed 10 Sep. 2020].

UNB (2020d). *Bangladesh wins People's Choice Award at Stockholm Junior Water Prize*. [Online] The Daily Star. Available at: https://www.thedailystar.net/bangladesh-wins-people-choice-award-stockholm-junior-water-prize-1951969 [Accessed 27 Aug. 2020].

Valor, G.B. (2020). *Professional information about meteorological conditions in the world OGIMET*. [Online] OGIMET. Available at: http://ogimet.com/resynops.phtml.en [Accessed 10 Sep. 2020].

WMO (2014). *COMISSION FOR CLIMATOLOGY FAQs | WMO*. [Online] Wmo.int. Available at: https://www.wmo.int/pages/prog/wcp/ccl/faqs.php [Accessed 23 Sep. 2020].

Chapter 4

Winter Climate Variability and Projections in Southern regions and Bangladesh

Mariam Hussain, Nusrat Sharmin

Bangladesh, a sub-tropical country, experiences extreme climate/weather events: floods, droughts, and tropical cyclones to adversely impacts people, properties, and country's economy. Despite of natural calamities, winter seasonality in December and January and its impacts due to climate changes have limited documentations. Thus, the current research aims to evaluate winter climatology by addressing historical status. The study site is focused on southern regions: Barishal and Patuakhali as coastal cities.

The data incorporates (daily) observations from Bangladesh Meteorological Department (1989 to 2015) and Ogimet (2016 to 2019). For 30 years, weather/climate variables: minimum and maximum winter temperature (°C) and rainfall (mm) are scrutinized to predict future winters. The statistical approach i.e. data mining are performed for trend, (linear and multi-linear) regression, descriptive statistics for climatological analysis. The results found that projections are significantly important to have accurate data from diverse observational stations.

Specifically, the multi-linear regression showed that incorporation of multiple observations improve winter projections. The paper also provides an illustration in socio-economical necessities how winter projected for current/future development works in southern regions. The reductions of winter seasonality affected in unemployment and biodiversity losses. In conclusion, the key findings and insights are important to utilize in future land-uses and livelihood managements and to suggest low-impact developments for future sustainability.

Introduction

A sub-tropical climate is prominent in Bangladesh representing summer, monsoon, autumn, late autumn, winter, and spring seasons. However, these variations are not prominent to observe because of irregular extreme natural disasters. A snapshot of climate scenarios is regularly documented in Bangladesh Bureau of Statistics (BBS). From these reports, extreme events, seasonal variations, and climates are summarized. For instance, statistics show for recent decades only four prominent seasons: pre-monsoon (Mar, Apr, and May), monsoon (Jun, Jul, and Aug), post-monsoon (Sep, Oct, and Nov), winter (Dec, Jan, and Feb) in Bangladesh (BBS, 2017). BBS also reports minimum temperature about 6°C recorded in Sitakunda and Faridpur from 2012 to 2015. On the other hand, southern regions of Bangladesh are coastal regions that usually experience tidal and regional floods. For last 5 years, such minimum temperature near coastal regions questions on winter seasonality and its variability across the country for which agricultural sectors and local people's livelihoods become concerned.

Moreover, growing population also contributes in changing agricultural and forest areas into developing the land-uses from villages to sub-urban and cities. Recent road constructions and development activities aided more to increase urban areas while causing bio-diversity losses and extreme disastrous impacts. Besides, meteorological extreme weather events - droughts or floods, coastal areas experiences tidal floods and shorter winter days. Yet, winter weather conditions in these regions are under-represented in literatures. Even though winter related research or reports are limited, news articles provide some recorded events and information that the country is experiencing. Dhaka tribune reported cold wave and dense fog events (Hossain, 2018). Fig. 1 shows an exemplary situation during winter that affect both city and village (elderly) people and children for coping winter. The resulted fog events and cold waves also badly hamper communication and transportations in leading accidents and deaths (Hossain, 2018; Paul, 2019; Regmi, 2019). These news and statistics provide equal importance comparing to flood or drought events with socio-economic and environmental concerns for investigating local situations.

Figure 1: Winter and Impacts in rural and major cities, Bangladesh (Photo: Hussain, 2018)

Several previous studies address on dry seasonal variability and its climatology for various applications. Bhuyan et al. (2014) studied temperature and winter variability in Bangladesh for 33 years from 1979 to 2012 where they concluded decreasing trends for rainfall and increasing trend (3.22 °C/ 100 year) on average except Dhaka. Hossain, Roy and Datta (2014) provided insights on spatial and temporal rainfall variability in south-west coastal regions from 1940 to 2007 using Mann-Kendall test in the time series data and showing the lowest recorded rainfall in their chosen sites. The weather/climate variables are also one of the key driving parameters in understanding river flows and salinity relationship. For instance, monsoon and winter periods and their impacts were under investigations for understanding residual currents and its effects on salinity distribution in Meghna Estuary incorporating meteorological variables (Hussain, Hossain, and Haque, 2012). Moreover, Shahid (2010) studied rainfall variability during wet and dry periods from 1958 to 2007 by Mann-Kendall trend test and concluded decreasing dry months in monsoon and pre-monsoon. Yet, their results followed conclusions on drought events based on dry or wet months.

These above studies are limited to enhance any discussions or understanding for winter variability in Bangladesh. However, the sub-tropical climate, total area in coastal regions, and upstream in the northern regions show distinct characteristics by their geological and geographical locations. The climate/weather events, socio-economic impacts, and limited literatures on winter variability provide a ground to explore any historical or climatological investigation aiding to the understanding our knowledge on climate change and its behaviors or patterns particularly for winter. Thus, in context of winter climate and extreme events, the current paper aims to consider several meteorological variables for understanding climate change, their trends and relationships to project future climate/weather patterns and for applying to socio-economic enhancement. The chapter outlines are methodology in section 2, results and discussions in section 3, applications in socio-economy in section 4, and concluding remarks with future directions in section 5.

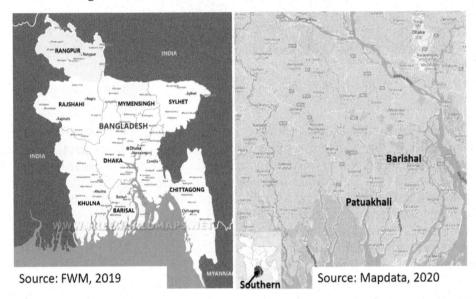

Source: FWM, 2019   Source: Mapdata, 2020

Figure 2: Study site: Barishal and Patuakhali in Southern regions (right panel) and Bangladesh (left panel)

Experimental Methodology

The investigation of winter climate is for the southern region, Bangladesh. Fig. 2 shows that southern regions are coastal areas and elevations are very close to the sea level. For example, Barishal and Patuakhali have elevations respectively 3 and 2 meter. In order to scrutinize winter climate scenarios, the studied variables are minimum and maximum temperature (°C) and rainfall (mm) for December and January for 30 years from 1989 to 2019. The obtained data is from Bangladesh Meteorological Department (BMD) for 1989 to 2015 and from Ogimet for 2016 to 2019 years. Table 1 summarizes geography and data details. The Ogimet is an open access data and found at www.ogimet.com. As observational stations provide daily summaries, this information is for several statistical analyses such as trend and pattern analysis, descriptive statistics, linear, and multiple linear regression (MLR). The statistical calculations and their findings are in section 3.

Table 1: Study sites information (a) Stations geographies (b) Data

a Stations	Latitude	Longitude	Elevation	b Data		
Dhaka	23.76667	90.38333	8m	**City Data:**	**Barishal**	**Patuakhali**
Mymensingh	24.71667	90.43333	18m	NA	Period	Source
Rajshahi	24.36667	88.7	23m	107	1989 to 2015	BMD
Rangpur	25.73333	89.23333	33m	61	1989 to 2015	BMD
Khulna	22.78333	89.53333	3m		2016 to 2019	Ogimet
Chittagonj	22.27	91.82	4m		2016 to 2019	Ogimet
Barisal	**22.75**	**90.36667**	**3m**			
Patuakhali	**22.33333**	**90.33333**	**3m**	**NA = Not available**		

Results

The results and discussion section explain and analyze trends or patterns by time series, linear regression (LR), and multiple linear regression (MLR) for evaluating winter season in southern region, Bangladesh. These investigations are experimented by trend and linear regression analysis for minimum and maximum temperature (°C) and rainfall. Figure 3, 4, and 5 represents these variables for Patuakhali and Barishal respectively. These boxplots clearly distinguish two different scenarios for the study regions in minimum and maximum temperature trends. For maximum temperature, fig. 3 indicates that there is no much difference for average maximum temperature between two areas for December and January months.

However, December month is warmer than January in both cities. Moreover, the minimum temperature shows Patuakhali is warmer than Barishal whereas December is warmer than January. These climatic trends explicitly reveal significant trends for winter mostly for minimum temperature.

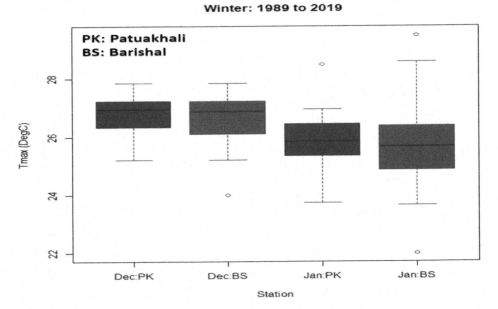

Figure 3: Climatic trends for maximum winter temperature (°C) in southern regions from 1989 to 2019

Similarly, rainfall is very low during winter seasons particularly in January. The average is almost no rainfall during winter except irregular rainfalls. These irregular events are extreme values that significantly affect lifestyles and livelihoods in these regions. As rainfall is one of the key inputs in agricultures for irrigational purposes, rainfall amount is also necessary to diagnose for winter seasons. Fig. 5 indicates rainfall time series in winter for 30 years. In dry season, few amount of rainfall might be helpful for irrigational systems in these regions. However, rainy conditions in winter might also create heavy low-level clouds in hindering sunspots. This might be difficult for people suffering from cold (shown in Fig. 1). Similarly, this condition might also form dense fog reducing visibilities in the early morning. Fig. 1 indicates how lower visibility might increase risks for highways and result in accidents. The lower visibilities would directly hamper in water and road transports as well as fisheries industries in the southern regions. Eventually, investigating winter season is worth enough to explore significant effects both in people's lives and in their properties.

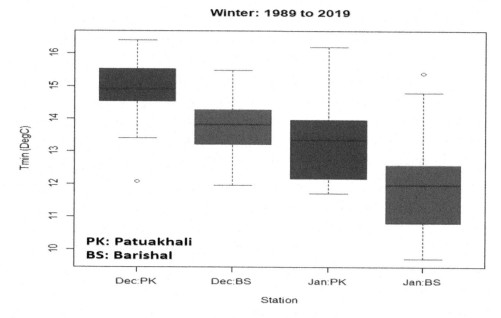

Figure 4: Similar to Fig. 3 but valid for minimum temperature (°C)

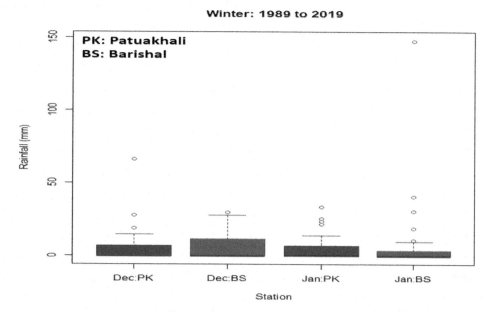

Figure 5: Similar to Fig. 3 but valid for rainfall (mm)

The linear trend analyses reveal several relationships from daily temperature to winter season for southern region. When the temperature is formulated monthly average data from daily summaries, there is no significant trends. However, the smoothed time series explicitly reveals increasing or decreasing trend respectively for Patuakhali and Barishal stations. Fig. 6 and 7 show maximum and minimum trends over 30 years. These trends indicate a weak increase or decrease relationship indicating a chaotic connection in climate. These results suggest for recent years that a strong non-linear interactions and uncertainties of climate in changing temperature. This result also opens discussion how these temperatures profiled in sub-tropical climate zones over time. Indirectly, these temperature behaviors prove how chaotic behaviors of atmosphere and climate are acting upon temperature between winter season and human induced activates.

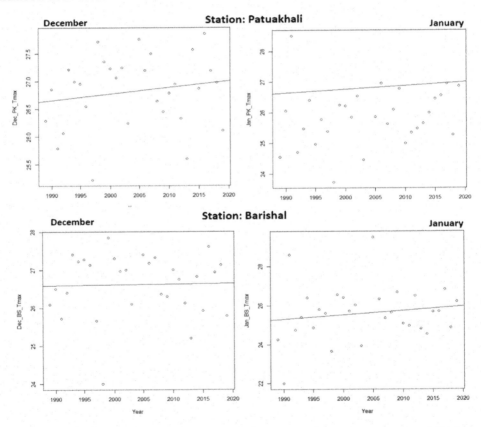

Figure 6: Linear regression for monthly averaged maximum temperature (°C) for Patuakhali (top panel) and Barishal (bottom panel) in winter (December and Janunary) from 1989 to 2019

74

One might argue for these statistical analyses and limited period for climate studies (30 years in the current study). The data from both stations is equally available from 1989 as Patuakhali as newly built station after liberation war. Another reason is missing values in the data (shown in Table 1b). The struggle in data analysis significantly underestimate the conclusions because of unavailable data. Therefore, the analysis limits for only 30 years. These LR results are able to infer a trend but are not strong for a greater conclusion. Therefore, the data size, accuracy of the ground observation, calculation method, and their intrinsic results refer to only specific sample size of the data. In order to generalize for greater areas of population, the numbers of quality data are equally important for a robust reference.

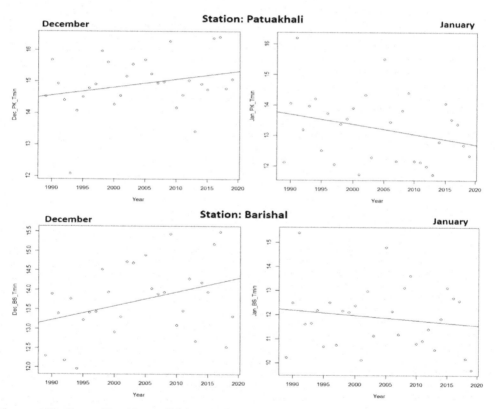

Figure 7: Similar to Fig. 6 but valid for minimum temperature (°C)

Most available information such as historical events and recorded observations are vital for finding key references. For instance, statistics of each station reveal significance for modelling future projections. Table 2 provides statistical analysis for southern regions that scrutinizes the probabilities in future winter projections. Firstly, table 2a indicates how diverse data are significant in increasing the reliabilities for statistical modeling. When the number of variables (temperature in this case) and observation sites are more (4) available, the prediction accuracy (R^2 = 0.44) is increases. This multi-linear regression (MLR) performs better than only LR. As the minimum temperature is becoming warmer, the MLR is also only for minimum temperature (Tmin). It also might infer that maximum temperature (Tmax) is not much influenced due to large-scale interactions between tropics to sub-tropics. Secondly, the descriptive statistics are also in table 2b. These values indicate the sample sizes are statistically significant inferring to entire population based on Tmin, Tmax, and rain (meteorological variables). As the descriptive statistics yield a normal distribution for each variable, this results are significant in MLR for future projections. Thus, winter season projects to be warmer in these regions due to increasing of Tmin.

Table 2: Statistical Analysis and Data Mining

(a) Multi-Linear Regression (MLR)

Models	Variables	R^2	Adjusted R^2
3	4 (station)	0.4404	0.3509
2	2	0.4017	0.3327
1	2	0.2275	0.1703
0	1	0.2205	0.1926

(b) Descriptive Statistics

Variables						
		Barishal			Patuakhali	
Stats	Rain	Tmax	Tmin	Rain	Tmax	Tmin
Minimum	0	15.8	6.5	0	15.4	7.4
Median	0	26.5	12.5	0	26.5	14
Mean	0.252	26.044	12.829	0.193	26.257	14.146
Mode	0	27	12	0	26.5	15
Maximum	63	31.5	21.4	36.6	32.3	22.2

Application in socio-economy

Winter season is an attraction for seasonal tourisms, travels, and fisheries that affect both livelihoods and economy in Southern region. Warmer winter indirectly influence waterbodies in Barishal Division. In a personal interview with Mr. Enamul Haque, a traveler and photographer, he recently visited Ramnabadh and Agunmokha River (Given in Fig. 8 and 9). He compares his childhood to recent years that rivers and channels are clear supporting fisheries. However, he concerns for recent constructions and infrastructures introduced in the division. As a danger zone for tropical cyclones, are development and infrastructures in coastal areas sustainable? How is the elevation suitable for heavy constructions? The waterbodies is also a concern for future water pollution that might cause extinctions of aquatic lives and diversity like Buriganga River. This eventually affects fishing trawlers losing their jobs. These scenarios raise issues on our preparedness to combat climate change. Therefore, projections for future winter climate is inevitable.

28 Jan 2019, Ramnabadh River || Patuakhali District || At 11.34 am. Photograph: Syed Enamul Haque

Figure 8: Livelihoods in winter and recent developments in Patuakhali, Bangladesh. (Photos Syed Enamul Haque)

River: Estuary/Channel to Agunmokha | Upozila: Rangabali (Union: Koraliya) | Patuakhali, Barisal, Bangladesh
Photo taken at 5.30 pm on 07 Feb 2019 by Syed Enamul Haque

Figure 9: Similar to Fig. 8 but valid for water ecosystems (Photos Syed Enamul Haque)

Winter climate also plays roles in livelihoods and land-use in southern regions. Specifically along with men, women in Patuakhali work in both local village markets (bazar), rice-mills and in agro-based activities (See Fig. 8). The changes in winter have impacts in their works. For example, fogy, cloudy, or cold waves cause the sun covering its light. The infrequent extreme incidents severely affect workers (mostly women). This eventually reduces their income source and struggles for family. Moreover, a warmer climate also affect biodiversity losses and medicinal plants in these regions. Specifically, Mr. Haque mentioned, "Haritaki (traditional plant) is becoming rare these days due to warmer winter" (shown in Fig. 11). He continued, "We dry this (Haritaki) seed in winter. Any sudden rain or fogs reduce our working time." These refer how changing winter are affecting their livelihoods, and source of treatments. Therefore, how do these people face biodiversity loss and unemployment due to temperature variability and change?

Figure 10: Women Participation in Local markets and Rice Mills, Patuakhali, Bangladesh (Photos Syed Enamul Haque)

Tree: *Haritaki* taken on 16 Feb. 2019 || Photograph: Syed Enamul Haque

Figure 11: Medicinal (spice) plants in endangered eco-systems (Photos Syed Enamul Haque)

Conclusion

In this paper, the winter climate is evaluated based on meteorological stations by addressing historical status in Bangladesh for 30 years data. Statistical methods such as multi-linear regression observe an increasing trend for minimum and maximum winter temperature (°C) in climatological analysis. From these analyses, the significance of data availability, quality, and accuracy are discussed for statistical modeling in winter climate projections. The analysis of descriptive statistics in the southern region explains normal distributions of sampled data that motivates predicting winter temperature for southern regions. The changes in temperature (winter season) have significant impacts in livelihoods and economy. Related development works also highly depend upon temperature change. These phenomena lead several future directions to generalize for the entire country. First, data mining is necessary to create database for accurate historical event for a platform applying Machine-Learning (ML) techniques. ML might incorporates more meteorological variables such as wind, relative humidity, cloud and solar radiation for advanced winter climate projections. Eventually, this study will help enhancing a tool for the winter season to understand the extreme weather events and mitigate the socio-economic impacts.

Acknowledgement: The first author likes to show her gratitude to Mr. Enamul Haque for providing photos and valuable information from his village. The authors also acknowledge supports by Bangladesh Meteorological Department for providing station data.

References

Abdul, D., Catharien, Q., Van Scheltinga, T., Fulco, Bangladesh, L., Plan, D. and Saha, T. (2016). *Recent changes in temperature and rainfall trends and variability over Bangladesh.* [Online] Conference on Climate Research: Gobeshona, pp.1–17. Available at: http://gobeshona.net/wp-content/uploads/2016/01/4.pdf [Accessed 4 Oct. 2020].

Bhuyan, M.D.I., Moniruzzaman, MD., Hossain, C.M.I., Islam, J. and Faruqe, S.B. (2014). Study of temperature and rainfall variability over

Bangladesh in winter season. *Journal of Science and Technology*, 4(1), pp.19–29.

Dhaka Tribune (2018). *Cold wave may continue till January 9.* [Online] Dhaka Tribune. Available at: https://www.dhakatribune.com/bangladesh/2018/01/07/cold-wave-may-continue-till-january-9/ [Accessed 4 Oct. 2020].

FWM (2019). *Bangladesh Political Map.* [Online] www.freeworldmaps.net. Available at: https://www.freeworldmaps.net/asia/bangladesh/political.html [Accessed 3 Oct. 2020].

Hossain, Md., Roy, K. and Datta, D. (2014). Spatial and Temporal Variability of Rainfall over the South-West Coast of Bangladesh. *Climate*, 2(2), pp.28–46.

Hossain, S.Z. (2018). *Bangladesh experiences record-breaking low temperature; improvement unlikely before 3 days.* [Online] Dhaka Tribune. Available at: https://www.dhakatribune.com/bangladesh/nation/2018/01/08/severe-cold-wave-country/ [Accessed 1 Oct. 2020].

Hussain, M.A., Hossain, M.A. and Haque, A. (2012). Hydro-Meteorological Impact on Residual Currents and Salinity Distribution at the Meghna Estuary of Bangladesh. *Coastal Environments: Focus on Asian Regions*, pp.88–105.

Paul, R. (2019). *Fifty dead as cold wave sweeps through Bangladesh.* [Online] The Star. Available at: https://www.thestar.com.my/news/world/2019/12/29/cold-snap-kills-50-in-bangladesh [Accessed 1 Oct. 2020].

Regmi, S.K. (2019). *Bangladesh: Cold wave - Information Bulletin - Bangladesh.* [Online] ReliefWeb. Available at: https://reliefweb.int/report/bangladesh/bangladesh-cold-wave-information-bulletin#:~:text=A%20cold%20wave%20is%20sweeping [Accessed 4 Oct. 2020].

Shahid, S. (2010). Rainfall variability and the trends of wet and dry periods in Bangladesh. *International Journal of Climatology*, 30(15), pp.2299–2313.

Shahid, S., Wang, X.-J., Harun, S.B., Shamsudin, S.B., Ismail, T. and Minhans, A. (2015). Climate variability and changes in the major cities of Bangladesh: observations, possible impacts and adaptation. *Regional Environmental Change*, 16(2), pp.459–471.

Srivastava, S.K., Sr., Sharma, D.A. and Sachdeva, K. (2017). An analysis, sensitivity and prediction of winter fog events using FASP model over Indo-Gangetic plains, India. *AGU Fall Meeting Abstracts*, [online] 51. Available at: https://ui.adsabs.harvard.edu/abs/2017AGUFM.A51A2019S/ abstract [Accessed 3 Oct. 2020].

Valor, G.B. (2020a). *Ogimet home page*. [Online] ogimet.com. Available at: http://ogimet.com/index.phtml.en [Accessed 30 Aug. 2020].

Chapter 5

Territories' adaptation to climate change and the effects of pandemics

Adel Ben Youssef, Mounir Dahmani, Séverine Borderon-Carrez

Introduction

Both climate change and pandemics have been shown to have huge impacts on spatial planning at different levels. Before the announcement of climate deregulation, the history of spatial planning was linked mainly to health crises. Major epidemics have made it possible to significantly change the way space and territory are organized and make them resilient to these recurring threats. Some epidemics have ended reigns, dynasties or regimes and heralded new eras leading to a reorganization of space and a renewed territorial organization. The global COVID-19 crisis, from the outset, emphasized the imbalances among territories and the need to take these into account in order to organize their response. Land use planning has returned to the fore in a spectacular way: spatial planning influences crisis management and can save lives or worsen health outcomes.

The management of both climate change and pandemics crises has undoubted territorial dimensions. First, on a global level, the first critical impacts of climate change have increased migration and caused huge displacements among populations. The International Organization for Migration (IOM) report on climate change states that "environmental refugees" exceeded total documented refugees from war and political persecution (IOM, 2008). Indeed, « As early as 1990 the Intergovernmental Panel on Climate Change (IPCC) noted that the greatest single impact of climate change might be on human migration—with millions of people displaced by shoreline erosion, coastal flooding and agricultural disruption. Since then, successive reports have argued that environmental degradation, and in particular climate change, is poised to become a major driver of population displacement—a crisis in the making »(IOM, 2008,p.9).

But to where do these migrants flee? Some studies highlight cities and megacities with access to water, food and health services the main reasons for their attraction. In Argentina, Chile and Brazil, immigrants are concentrated mostly in large cities. In Argentina, it is estimated that 70% of migrants reside in the Metropolitan Area of Buenos Aires, in Chile 65% reside in the Metropolitan Area of Santiago, while the majority of migrants to Brazil live in São Paulo, followed by Rio de Janeiro and Paraná (Warn and Adamo, 2014).

Thus, we observe that, first, climate change is causing global migration and, second, that the COVID-19 crisis has resulted in some interesting population evolutions. This is leading to new mapping and territorial dynamics.

Once the COVID-19 pandemic began affecting decisions about study, work, medical treatment, travel and food supplies, land management became vital. The COVID-19 pandemic serves as a test of the shortcomings, strengths and weaknesses of past land use planning policies around the world.

The aim of this short paper is to highlight five trends revealed by the COVID pandemic and the climate change crisis related directly or indirectly to land use planning. It studies the relationship between concentration of productive and social activities, the territory's health network, digitalization of the economy and future mobility projects, and the need to move to healthier production. It concludes with some recommendations for future regional planning policies.

The risks of concentrating productive activities

The concentration of productive activities is a high-risk factor that requires cities to become more sustainable, smart and circular. The global health crisis has revealed the limits of the current model of concentration of activities in overpopulated and highly polluted territories: Wuhan, the Paris region, New York, San Paolo, Milan, London, etc.. Many studies find a correlation between air pollution and the impact of COVID-19 (Travaglio *et al.*, 2020; Cole, 2020 ; Suresh, 2020) and some consider that pollution has exacerbated the spread of the virus. Hippocrates said, "If you're sick on your own, you must have eaten something bad. But if several of us are sick, it is because the air is not good. So, we have to change the air, make it circulate". The idea that air quality mattered persisted up to the 19th century. Haussman and Napoleon III tried to clean Paris up through architectural and town planning projects that promoted better public hygiene (Chevallier, 2010).

The limits of super-concentrated cities and public transport systems have become clear. However, the emphasis on climate change considered displacement of populations over the long term. In contrast, the recent pandemic has resulted in waves of city dwellers around the world fleeing cities for the countryside in the search for better sanitary conditions. These population displacements from large cities to the countryside is unprecedented in modern history. However, this redistribution of populations across territories revealed the constraints on the organization of logistics to provide basic services and the limitations of the current model.

Some studies of the phenomenon of a slow, but progressive urban exodus since the 1970s in France, emphasize that it has multiple consequences for demography, social life, housing and mobility, agriculture and the environment, which are poorly understood (Merlin, 2009). In France, regional imbalances have emerged, with some territories accumulating services and others deprived of services. The corollary of this is that rural areas were emptied of their medical resources.

The old model of territorial organization led to the establishing of a logistics chain oriented towards large cities to the detriment of the remaining territory. Around the world, travel restrictions have meant that supply chains have had to be reorganized and cope with the partial shutdown of international trade. The search for local products and local services to compensate for imported products and services has led to a resurgence of the idea of efficient local economies. Territorial specialization and transport and transfer of services and goods should become typical of the past, making circular local development a must for territorial development.

Williams (2019) in her paper argues the importance of the circular economy on the spatial planning perspective, emphasizing the need to make more physical space in cities through planning instruments and involvement of circular economy, and transform cities to circular cities. Cities should be organized as a network of "villages". The new city will be a chance and a challenge in the same time, since the mitigation and adaptation strategies as regard of climate change impacts and environmental protection (Lai, 2017). Social distancing in order to prevent the spread of COVID-19 has enabled creation of less density in the cities, smart working and balanced spatial distribution of activities. Lai (2020, p.241) states that COVOD-19 should serve as a lesson to "drive towards innovative theoretical and technical visions concerning categories such as land take, soil sealing, intensive versus extensive urbanization, transportation networks, carbon capture and storage, and, ultimately, environmental, social and economic sustainability".

First, the COVID-19 crisis questions the concentration of productive and social activities and the for spatial planning to focus on peripheral areas to promote a circular economy based on short supply chains and smart and sustainable cities.

The health map to promote regional planning

The COVID-19 pandemic has renewed interest in the health map and coverage of territories by health facilities. Migration is often based on maximizing survival chances by fleeing from risky places and increasing proximity to health facilities. In this context, there are striking inequalities with 'medical deserts' clearly discernible. For instance, some regions had no hospital facilities, no intensive care facilities and no ventilators or other essential equipment. In some cases, including New York, the military set up field hospitals and, in almost all countries, patients were moved long distances to relieve the pressure on the hardest hit areas.

The health map needs to be reviewed. Provision of health facilities cannot follow a pure market logic and, across the world, public health provision is an issue (Chung, 2020). Provision of public health cannot be based purely on economic reasoning. Also, the countries suffering the greatest health crises are that have reduced public health sector spending the most over the past two decades, that is, Italy, England, the US, Brazil, etc., or which have ignored health provision. Without the engagement of civil society, the momentum provided by international solidarity, and without last-minute interventions the situation could have become catastrophic.

The ageing population is leading to a reconsideration of the health map and its network in every territory. A representative of Silver told us that « the COVID-19 crisis emphasized the daily issues that older people face in rural and mountainous areas due to the lack of services. The Silver Economy sector has demonstrated its capacity to assist the most vulnerable ones. The situation encourages reflexion on regional policies to support this crucial sector in our territories» (Interreg Europe, 2020). Living close to a good health care facility is a necessity for older people and it is clear that the decision to move to an urban center is sometimes dictated by access to hospitals and other health care establishments. A redistribution of the population will require some replanning of the health map and provision of university hospitals. Relevant health care policies could increase the attractiveness of some areas.

Scott (2020) shows how the COVID-19 crisis has caused great inequalities and spatial inequalities across cities and regions in matter of health. The most vulnerable people were older people. The solution of society for an elderly population has often been the predetermined separation - residential care units, pension villages, nursing homes. In this matter health needs to be restructured and to put more effort in creation of adequate health services for population of all ages. Further Scott (2020), states that messages such as stay home has been meaning for homeless people. A recent report in The Lancet highlights the challenges of coping with Covid-19 outbreaks in Brazil. "In the favelas, conditions are crowded and access to clean water is limited. In such circumstances, social distancing and hand-washing are virtually impossible" (Burki, 2020, p. 547).

Second, the crisis highlights the need to think about spatial planning in relation to the health map and to take more account of the so-called "silver economy". Demographic transition has an important effect on regional planning and health care must be part of this planning.

The consequences for the territory of increased digitization

COVID-19 has validated and accelerated the digital trajectory. Use of digital technologies increased during the pandemic: work, leisure, study, social life, health, shopping was all enabled by digital platforms. In the space of a few days, people became dependent on Zoom to enable their social and work interactions. Many individuals who had never participated on an online seminar (webinar), never participated in a virtual meeting, never made an online purchase became champions of online services and questioned the need for unnecessary trips, unnecessary interactions, unnecessary meetings etc.

In France, in eight weeks, queues at post offices and social services offices disappeared and online money transfer solutions which had been in abeyance for 20 years were put in place. Traders who had never used a keyboard began selling online and organized their logistics accordingly. Suddenly we all went online.

COVID-19 is leading to a rethinking of our lifestyles and increasing digitization. It has shown very clearly that a switch to online services is both necessary and urgent. This will involve infrastructure improvements (in particular optical fiber), coverage of the entire territory and a rethinking of the physical facilities to enable to switch to digital.

For example, many universities across the world will switch to E-learning in September 2020.

The implications are huge: no more need for university residences and need for fewer means of transport; however, the savings derived should be used to ensure fast broadband connections for students, provision of adequate equipment, space for working close to their homes and more library facilities. The increase of the level of digital skills positively influences students' performance (Ben Youssef et al. 2020). This would allow local populations to study close to their families and ensure more balanced territorial development.

For traders, logistics chains will need to be reorganized as online sales continue to grow, which will require secure transactions and payments methods and efficient logistics platforms. There will be no need to rent premises in a city to set up a business. The impact on office space will be huge and especially in the context of large international megacities. The impact on land use planning will be unprecedented. Many workers will be able to work remotely which will reduce migration to cities driven by employment. State services will be affected and will require rationalization and a focus on essential functions. It is estimated that 80% of state services could go online. The most difficult part of the process is starting it; once started, nothing will stop it. The COVID-19 pandemic has promoted this start process.

COVID-19 has accelerated the use of innovation and digital technologies also in the healthcare system. Healthcare in the future needs to be focused in the investment on innovation and digitalization (Barnes, 2020), since robots, sensors, artificial intelligence, blockchain and broadband networks provide components for monitoring and managing the personal health care of the most vulnerable patients remotely in the home environment (Rahman et al. 2019).

Third, technology is having a strong impact on our territories. COVID will greatly accelerate the digitalization of companies. However, digital transformation is an opportunity to rethink the territorial development model and our priorities. It is a unique opportunity to break free of old paradigms, without subscribing to a totalitarian paradigm.

The fight against climate change and quality of the environment and life are the priorities in post-COVID-19 land use planning

COVID-19 has given the world an 'ecological break. Some suggest the establishing of an interactive map to remind us and to which we can contribute[1]. This ecological break brought a realization of how much humans are overwhelming nature and the latter's capacity to reclaim its territory. Former near-extinct varieties of fish appeared in different oceans and rivers; turtles were able to lay and hatch their eggs undisturbed, butterflies appeared in their tens of thousands in city centers etc. The flora and fauna breathed during this ecological break while human beings enjoyed quieter, less frenzied and less polluted living environments and were able to observe their surrounding biodiversity.

1   https://globalpause.ushahidi.io/views/map

Pedestrians and cyclists returned to city centers. COVID-19 underlined that our territory is shared and that to survive our natural resources need our ecological footprint to be reduced. Future development should take account of these aspects and translate them into active policies. The Thai government has decided to close its national parks for several months a year to allow nature to regenerate – one of the lessons of COVID-19.[2] King and Krizek (2020) emphasize the importance of encouraging walking and cycling activities by using creating future pedestrian and cycling trails. The clean public transport should be encouraged by making buses and and environmentally-friendly (De Vos, 2020).

A change in the habits of citizens was noticed during lockdown in many countries worldwide (Lai et al 2020; Ben Youssef et al. 2020). Social distancing has enabled working online, conferencing online, shoping online, exploring tourism online and other related activities has shift online during the lockdown. As activities has shift online and the travel has been in a halt, there has been a decrease in carbon emissions and was noticed an improvement in the air quality (Ben Youssef, 2020).

Further, the innovation and the digitalization are the key for the reduction of carbon emissions. Ben Youssef (2020) states that significant technological change and the introduction of several new digital technologies which could allow radical transformations and the reduction of carbon emissions.

Preserving wild natural places and reducing pollution are essential to avoid future pandemics. Changing behavior related to the exploitation of resources is fundamental for a biological balance and food security. These concerns, which COVID-19 has highlighted, need to be translated into land use planning. An ambitious climate change policy should preserve our coastlines and our natural resources and encourage citizens to prepare for these adaptations. The COVID-19 crisis will be salutary if it leads to a reduction in uncontrolled development and increased sustainable development.

---

2 https://www.ulyces.co/news/la-thailande-va-fermer-ses-parcs-naturels-plusieurs-mois-par-an-pour-que-la-nature-se-regenere/

Fourth, development models need to take account of nature, the climate and biodiversity. The COVID-19 pandemic has shown us that the destruction of nature is damaging our food and health security and this destruction is reversible if the political will exists.

The agricultural map of the territory and the need for a return to more organic agricultural land

During the crisis, the European Commission published two strategies for 2030 – related to biodiversity and agriculture. The objective of these strategies in combination is to restore biodiversity and return to organic farming which will have a major impact on human health. The COVID-19 pandemic has highlighted the link between a poor diet and health (Nutri-Net, 2020). A return to peasant farming will change the dynamics in rural populations and could reduce migration.

In this context, the strategies propose to transform "at least 30% of European lands and seas into protected areas managed in an efficient way and by ensuring that at least 10% of the agricultural surface consists of topographical features of high diversity organic" (European Commission, May 20, 2020). The good news is that "the actions planned for the protection, sustainable use and restoration of nature will economically benefit local communities, creating jobs and sustainable growth. Funding of € 20 billion per year will be made available for biodiversity through various sources, including EU funds and national and private funding "(European Commission, May 20, 2020)."

The aim of this short note was to summarize the effects of the COVID-19 pandemic on current economic and social development models and the repercussions for land use planning policy. In the space available, we were able to discuss only four aspects. The consensus that COVID-19 has been 'a trend accelerator' provides a better understanding of the challenges we face in the 21st century. We must use this opportunity to rethink land use planning. Dismantling large metropolises, ensuring environmental quality in cities, promoting a circular and local economy, changing the priorities related to digital equipment, preserving critical natural capital and preparing citizens to adapt to climate change are among the many priorities that must be addressed in future land use plans.

References

Barnes, S. J. (2020). Information management research and practice in the post-COVID-19 world. International Journal of Information Management, 102175.

Ben Youssef, A. (2020) "How Industry 4.0 can contribute to combatting Climate Change?", Revue d'Economie Industrielle (French Industrial Economics Review) (Rank 3), June 2020, vol.169.

Ben Youssef, A., Dahmani, M and Ragni, L. 2020. "Technologies de l'information et de la communication, compétences numériques et performances académiques des étudiants," GREDEG Working Papers 2020-25, Groupe de REcherche en Droit, Economie, Gestion (GREDEG CNRS), Université Côte d'Azur, France.

Ben Youssef, A., Zeqiri, A., Dedaj, B. "Short and Long Run Effects of COVID-19 on the Hospitality Industry and the Potential Effects on Jet Fuel Markets". IAEE Energy Forum, May 2020, Covid-19 Issue 2020, p. 121-124.

Brown O., Migration and Climate Change, International Organization for Migration, Geneva, 2008.

Burki, T. (2020). Covid-19 in Latin America. The Lancet Infectious Diseases, 20(5), 247–248. https://doi.org/10.1016/S1473-3099(20)30303-0

Chevallier F., Le Paris moderne, Presses universitaires de Rennes, 2010.

Chung A., Une Pandémie qui met en lumière les injustices sociales, in The Conversation, mai 2020.

Cole M. et al. (2020), Air Pollution Exposure and Covid-19 in Dutch Municipalities, Environmental and Resources Economics, august 2020.

De Vos, J. (2020). The effect of COVID-19 and subsequent social distancing on travel behavior. Transportation Research Interdisciplinary Perspectives, 5(100121). http://dx.doi.org/10.1016/j.trip.2020.100121

King, D.A., Krizek, K.J. (2020) The power of reforming streets to boost access for human scaled vehicles. Transportation Research Part D: Transport and Environment, 83, 102336. https://doi.org/10.1016/j.trd.2020.102336

Lai, S., Leone, F. & Zoppi, C. (2017). Anthropization processes and protection of the environment: An assessment of land cover changes in Sardinia, Italy. Sustainability, 9(12, 2174), 19 pp. https://doi.org/10.3390/su9122174

Lai, S., Leone, F., Zoppi, C. (2020). Covid-19 and spatial planning. A few issues concerning public policy. Journal of Land Use, Mobility and Environment.

Merlin P, Exode urbain: de la ville à la campagne, Les Etudes de la Documentation Française (France) fre no. 5303, 2009.

Nutri-Net Study, EREN, Inserm U1153 / Inra U1125 / Cnam / Université Paris 13, from 2009 : https://etude-nutrinet-sante.fr/article/view/330-COVID-19---Nouveaux-questionnaires-NutriNet-Santé-:-la-recherche-en-santé-publique-a-besoin-de-vous-

Rahman M.A., Rashid M.M., Le Kernec J., Philippe B., Barnes S.J., Fioranelli F....Imran M. A secure occupational therapy framework for monitoring cancer patients' quality of life. Sensors. 2019;19(23):5258

Scott, M. (2020). Covid-19, Place-making and Health. Planning Theory & Practice, 1–6. doi:10.1080/14649357.2020.1781445

Silver SME, How the Silver Economy faces the COVID-19 crisis?, Interreg Europ, 24/04/20.

Suresh A. et all., Diagnostic Comparison of Changes in Air Quality over China before and during the COVID-19 Pandemic, 2020.

Travaglio M and al. (2020), Links between air pollution and COVID-19 in England, MRC Toxicology Unit, University of Cambridge, april 2020.

Warn E and Adamo SB (2014), The Impact of climate change : Migration and Cities in South America, IOM, vol 63(2), 2014.

Williams, J. (2019). Circular cities. Urban Studies. doi:10.1177/0042098018806133

Part III
Re-calibrating Economics

Chapter 6
Changing Role of Economics

Amber Leversedge

Introduction

The capitalist economic system is entrenched in most countries across the globe and has dramatically affected humans' perception and relationship with the environment and each other (Næss, 2015). The main features of capitalism involve the promotion of competition and the free market with the main priority being profit maximization and growth (Laamanen et al., 2018). In the capitalist system there is freedom of enterprise and consumer choice with minimal government intervention (Laamanen et al., 2018). Although capitalism has influenced rapid innovation and growth leading to sophisticated development and technological breakthroughs not everyone has benefited from this system and it has heavily influenced the most catastrophic crisis our world faces today (Næss, 2015; Kay et al., 2016; Borzaga et al., 2019).

Relentless growth has led to the exploitation and degradation of our natural environment and produced negative externalities, most notably greenhouse gases which contribute to the greenhouse effect leading to climatic changes (Rockström et al., 2009; Dietz and O'Neill, 2013). In 1979, the First World Climate Conference provided evidence that the significant rise in carbon dioxide emissions had been caused by anthropogenic sources (White, 1979). Yet, since the conference temperatures have continued to rise, and significant action to minimise greenhouse gas emissions has not been taken. These climatic changes are affecting every society in a multitude of different ways, from disturbing food production to the introduction of different diseases and pests to the destruction caused by the increasing frequency and severity of natural disasters (Rockström et al.,

2009; Dietz and O'Neill, 2013). According to Steffen et al. (2015) we have surpassed the safe levels of climate change, biodiversity loss, shifts in nutrient cycles (nitrogen and phosphorus), and land use which are four of the nine planetary boundaries. Crossing these boundaries increases the risk of unprecedented irreversible environmental change (Steffen et al., 2015; Fernandez-Mena et al., 2016).

In addition to a variety of environmental issues, capitalism has contributed to a number of social issues. Inequality has risen polarising minority groups in society as the majority power and wealth is held by a minute concentration of people including political and corporate elites (Kay et al., 2016; Laamanen et al., 2018). Capitalism has influenced these disparities and loss of social cohesion as it encourages individualist behaviour and competition over cooperation (Kay et al., 2016). These inequalities may be exacerbated in the future because the poorest in society are at the greatest risk from climate change and environmental destruction as they are the most vulnerable lacking adequate wealth and resources for adaption (Wilson, 2007).

Systemic change and radical transformation at each level of governance is desperately needed to combat these issues, including: reforming the monetary and financial system, changing values and the way we measure progress to account for scarcity and limits to growth, redistributing wealth, and major alterations to the production process and consumption patterns (Dietz and O'Neill, 2013). The following chapter will explore solutions to improve resilience and prosperity focusing on the social and solidarity economy (SSE) and the circular economy (CE) using case studies of organisations that have implemented these strategies as supporting evidence. However, it is important to note, the approaches discussed will only be effective if the economic system undergoes a transformative change as the current capitalist system is a barrier to their expansion. It should also be acknowledged that many changes could be made to the current economic system to reduce inequality whilst ensuring environmental protection which cannot be covered in the chapter. Firstly, the SSE will be discussed to investigate how the economy can be altered to improve social sustainability. The SEE refers to a variety of organizations including: social enterprises, foundations, associations, cooperatives and mutual benefit societies and aims to improve wellbeing and meet the needs of the community (Borzaga et al., 2019). Secondly, the CE will be explored to discover how the economy can be transformed to progress environmental sustainability. The CE attempts to alter the current linear take-make-waste system to a closed loop system with a central aim of both restoration and regeneration (Geissdoerfer et al., 2017).

Social and Solidarity Economy

The SSE is gaining interest at a local level as there is an increasing recognition that there should be a greater focus on cooperation over competition with the needs of the community at the centre (Pearce, 2003). The main features of organizations within the SSE is that they focus on improving quality of life, are often bottom up and have a large proportion of volunteers (Borzaga et al., 2019). In addition, multiple stakeholders are involved in the ownership of the organisation, the decision-making process aims to be inclusive and it is imperative these organisations focus on the interests of their members, wider community and society (Borzaga et al., 2019). This people centred approach aims to provide long term security, and innovation and entrepreneurship in reaction to societal needs (Borzaga et al., 2019). The SSE should help to minimize inequalities as collective ownership of the means of production means allocation and distribution of resources should be fair (Utting, 2015). Care, justice and compassion are important elements of the SSE with high job satisfaction, outstanding quality services and low profitability meaning the risk of exploitations and asymmetric information is significantly reduced (Hansmann, 1988; Borzaga et al., 2019). The SSE works to improve resilience as the organisations are not profit focused they do not depend on the state of the economy meaning they can support the community during an external crisis (Kay at al., 2016; Borzaga et al., 2019).

Social Enterprise

Social enterprises (SEs) are a type of organisations that form part of the SSE. SEs have no legal definition but are thought of as organisations whose primary aim is to promote social or environmental sustainability as oppose to profit (Pearce, 2003; OECD, 2019). There are three dimensions to SEs: social, entrepreneurial and governance as displayed in figure 1 (PwC, 2018). SEs encompass a variety of forms with different goals, including: welfare provision, education platforms, community based, the inclusion of disadvantaged groups in the work force, and reducing environmental damage (Borzaga et al., 2019).

Amsterdam in the Netherlands has a growing number of SEs whose growth is facilitated by government support. The number of SEs in Amsterdam has risen from 2000-2500 to 5000-6000 and jobs in the sector have risen by more than 60% from 2010 to 2016 (McKinsey, 2016). A specific example is Woodworks which is a shop producing high quality wood products and is a work integration social enterprise (Blonk et al., 2020). The objective of this organisation is to provide employment to those suffering from mental health issues or mild intellectual disabilities (Blonk et al., 2020). Therefore, the organisation's goal is to enhance social capital and reduce inequalities. Woodworks is designed around care and building relationships to support its employees, for instance, working hours are shorter and more flexible (Blonk et al., 2020). This SE helps to create a more inclusive and accepting environment and make all individuals feel respected and appreciated helping to eliminate any associated stigma of those with mental health issues or intellectual disabilities (Blonk et al., 2020). This improves the self-esteem and quality of life of employees as they feel as if they are contributing to society and training and education helps to build their skills (Block et al., 2020).

This demonstrates the importance of these organisations as they shift the focus from growth, profit maximising and consumerism to a more care-based economy assisting the local community by reducing inequalities and injustices (Pearce, 2003; Dietz and O'Neill, 2013). The core impacts of SEs have a mutually beneficial relationship. However, these organisations have some drawbacks as they tend to have low profitability they usually require government assistance to help with the set up and operation which according to Kay et al. (2016) risks losing the essence of SE (McKinsey, 2016). The lack of legal definition is a major barrier to the growth of SEs as it means they are less recognisable which could limit public support (Kay et al., 2016; OECD, 2019). In addition, it is difficult to monitor the impact and progress of SEs the social and environmental outcomes are challenging to quantify (Kay et al., 2016).

Cooperatives

Cooperatives are defined as a group of volunteers that through democratic decision making and cooperation equally own an enterprise to achieve their social, cultural and economic needs and the needs of the wider community (Borgaza and Sforzi, 2014). All members of cooperatives are involved in the decision making process meaning they have high levels of cooperation and coordination (Bretos and Marcuello, 2017). Cooperatives tend to network with other local organisations to cement stability and transfer knowledge and resources (Borgaza and Sforzi., 2014). The main goal of these organisations is to serve the community not growth and profit which enables them to be more resilient and adaptable to external changes (Borzaga et al., 2019).

The Brazilian government have ensured cooperatives are incorporated into their national development plan helping to encourage their expansion (Vicari, 2014). A specific example of this is Cooperativa de Pequenos Produtores Agroextrativistas de Lago do Junco (COPPALJ) which is a farming cooperative mainly based around producing babaçu nuts and selling oil in various markets (Vicari, 2014). This organisation is situated in Maranhão and has 107 members (over half of which are women) and focuses on empowering women in the workforce and reducing inequalities (Vicari, 2014). COPPALJ contributes to social sustainability be tackling gender issues and employees believe the organisation has had positive impacts at both a household and community level (Vicari, 2014). The cooperative promotes participation, democracy, and social inclusion by enabling all members to take part in board meetings, offering training to employees to develop their skills, and splitting the remaining income equally (Vicari, 2014).

This evidence shows cooperatives help empower local communities by uniting people through cooperation and inclusivity enhancing social capital. Even so, there are some barriers to the expansion of cooperatives which limit their influence. If cooperatives become too large this may undermine the democratic and participatory nature of cooperatives as ensuring each individual contributes equally becomes more complex (Bretos and Marcuello, 2017). The decision making process can be slow and inefficient for cooperatives as a large number of people are involved which can reduce their effectiveness (Bretos and Marcuello, 2017). Another barrier to the development of cooperatives is that they are dependent on a collaborative and trusting spirit and if a region does not possess these values it is a lengthy and difficult process to encourage the establishment of these organisations (Luzarraga, 2008).

Circular Economy

The concept of a CE has attracted large amount of attention in recent years from governments, policymakers, academics and organisations on a regional, national and global scale as it takes a holistic and practical approach to solving issues related to scarce resources, production, consumption, and waste (Brennan et al., 2015; Stahel, 2016; Geissdoerfer et al., 2017). Ultimately the aim of a CE is to eliminate waste and promote more efficient resource use, reducing both consumption and pollution and achieving long term resilience (Geissdoerfer et al., 2017). CE models involve reusing, remanufacturing and repairing the good or recycling components to converting outdated goods into new products, as displayed in figure 3 (Stahel, 2016). Within CE there are a number of schools of thought including cradle-to-cradle (McDonough and Braungart, 2002), regenerative design (Lyle, 1994) and industrial ecology (Fernandez-Mena et al., 2016) to name a few.

Industrial Ecology

Industrial ecology is a school of thought within the CE and is based on scientific research and discoveries of the relationship between industrial society which is viewed as a system and the environment (Fernandez-Mena et al., 2016). This approach aims enhance natural capital to keep the flow of materials in a loop reducing the need to exploit finite resources (Fernandez-Mena et al., 2016; Saavedra et al., 2018). Industrial ecology can involve a variety of different strategies including Life Cycle Assessment, Substance Flow Analysis and Industrial Symbiosis Analysis (Fernandez-Mena et al., 2016). Industrial Symbiosis is based on biology and how unrelated organisms share energy, resources and information in a mutually beneficial relationship (Chertow, 2000). The industrial system can use this concept by collaborating with businesses and exchanging materials, energy and knowledge to improve efficiency and environmental sustainability (Chertow, 2000).

China produces the largest amount of chemicals globally which have led to a number of negative externalities (Yune et al., 2016). To combat this issue Eco-Industrial Parks have been created which are an industrial ecology strategy (Yune et al., 2016). These parks have economic, social and environmental benefits as they cluster businesses encouraging them to coordinate and communicate with fellow business and the local community sharing knowledge and resources improving both efficiency and environmental responsibility (Chertow, 2000). One of the most notable examples is the Shanghai Chemical industrial Park (SCIP) which began functioning in 2005 and consists of about 40 manufacturing firms (Yune et al., 2016). Some of the environmental benefits include utility sharing, such as wastewater treatment parks as high-quality efficient equipment can be bought as the costs are shared between the organisations (Yune et al., 2016). In addition, knowledge sharing has produced a sophisticated online system which can detect over 100 chemicals to assist with environmental monitoring which occurs monthly (Yune et al., 2016). Eco-Industrial Parks enable the local government to have more control over the industry ensuring businesses comply to regulations (Yune et al., 2016).

This indicates industrial ecology reduces negative externalities as by understanding material and energy flows organisations are able to conserve resources by mirroring natural systems (Saavedra et al., 2018). However, it is debatable whether improving efficiency is a significant enough action to combat environmental issues and whether more emphasis should be placed on community involvement. Perhaps combining industrial ecology with other strategies would make it more effective at reducing environmental damage. In order for industrial ecology strategies to be successful there needs to be collaboration between many stakeholders including business, government, and policymakers which can be complicated and time consuming to coordinate as values and priorities may differ (Saavedra et al., 2018).

Cradle to Cradle

The cradle-to-cradle (C2C) framework is based on natural closed loop systems meaning the whole life cycle is taken into account and at the end of the products life the materials can be reused or can biodegrade (Bakker et al., 2010). This creates a circular flow of materials meaning in the technical cycle the materials from one production process are reused for another product and in the biological cycle materials can be reabsorbed into the cycle (McDonough and Braungart, 2002). According to McDonough and Braungart (2002) the framework is centred around three principles: waster equals food (waste should not exist as it is inefficient and harmful), use current solar income (renewable energy should be utilised) and celebrate diversity (appreciating that the design should be adapted different environments and economies).

In 2005 a C2C certification for products was created with a stringent list of criteria for five different categories (basic, bronze, silver, gold, platinum) (Bjørn and Hauschild, 2018). This helps to give organisations recognition for developing an environmentally sustainable product. Trigema is a clothing store based in Germany with C2C Silver certified clothing products (Bjørn and Hauschild, 2018). The clothes are made using organic cotton and no toxic products are used meaning at the end of life the product is biodegradable or recyclable adhering to C2C principles (Bjørn and Hauschild, 2018). The product is also of high quality making it durable and a longer lifetime reduces the resource use and waste produced.

The evidence shows that the C2C framework is both ecologically responsible and resilient in the long term as it considers limits to growth and ensures materials aren't overexploited (McDonough and Braungart, 2002). On the other hand, there is a risk that this concept may not be feasible as creating a truly C2C product is extremely challenging, even the Platinum certification for C2C does not mean the product completely follows each C2C principle in every aspect of the products life cycle (Bjørn and Hauschild, 2018). The expansion of a circular economy from a bottom up level may be limited if employees lack the technical and economic knowledge to alter business models to a closed loop (Stahel, 2016). In addition, the C2C approach relies on the consumer to dispose of the product as the end of its lifetime in an sustainable way, yet consumers may not be educated on this matter, there should be more focus in the role of consumption in this framework (Reay et al., 2011).

Conclusion

Economic systems are constantly evolving and with increasing recognition and understanding that the current capitalist system has contributed to a range of social and environmental problems it is crucial that the system is transformed. The SSE and CE are important components to the transition to a more resilient and socially and environmentally sustainable world. However, many significant changes are needed to make this shift and without these reforms the impact of the SSE and CE may be limited.

Stratan (2017) states that there should be more focus on integrating social impact in addition to CE principles in business models enabling them to respond to a diverse range of social and environmental issues. Some of these organisations already exist such as the Rainbow Junk-tion community café based in Leeds, England. This organisation uses SSE strategies as it is volunteer run and provides food which is pay as you feel (Rainbow Junk-tion, 2020). This improves social sustainability as it enables people to get a nutritious meal for an extremely low cost helping to support the poorest in society and reducing inequalities (Rainbow Junk-tion, 2020). In addition, the café operation is based on circular economy principles as the food is gathered from supermarkets leftover food which they would otherwise throw out (Rainbow Junk-tion, 2020). This improves environmental sustainability as food is not wasted but instead used to produce another product, reducing waste and overexploitation of resources (Rainbow Junk-tion, 2020). This shows that sustainable business models are flexible and there are many methods which can be used to enhance social and natural capital.

To establish the importance of the SSE and CE governments and policymakers must help facilitate the growth and development of initiatives that encompass these concepts. The support could be in the form of grants or subsidies to incentivise activities that benefit society and the environment and taxes on those that are harmful (Stahel, 2016). To encourage the development of these organisations education and training programmes could be established to encourage resilient thinking.

Research and innovation are needed across multiple disciplines from economists, to scientist to environmentalists to assess the viability and feasibility of these concepts and create strategies to cement their implementation (Stahel, 2016).

Overall, rethinking the current economic system and providing platforms and support for the develop of alternatives such as the SSE and CE is fundamental in providing long term resilience and prosperity. These approaches will assist in changing our values to build communities and societies based on respect and stewardship towards the environment and each other.

References

Bakker, C. A., Wever, R., Teoh, C., & De Clercq, S. 2010. Designing Cradle to Cradle products: a reality check. International Journal of Sustainable Engineering. 3(1), pp. 2-8.

Bjørn, A., and Hauschild, M. Z. 2018. Cradle to Cradle and LCA. In: Hauschild, M., Rosenbaum, R., and Olsen, S. eds. Life Cycle Assessment. [Online]. Cham, Switzerland: Springer, pp. 605-631. [Accessed 26 August 2020]. Available from: https://link.springer.com/chapter/10.1007/978-3-319-56475-3_25#citeas

Blonk, L., Huijben, T., Bredewold, F., and Tonkens, E. 2020. Balancing care and work: a case study of recognition in a social enterprise. Disability and Society. 35(6), pp. 972-992.

Borzaga, C., Salvaori, G., and Bodini, R. 2019. Social and Solidarity Economy and the Future of Work. Journal of Entrepreneurship and Innovation in Emerging Economies. 5(1), pp. 37-57.

Borzaga, C., and Sforzi, J. 2014. Social capital, cooperatives and social enterprises. In Christoforou, A., and Davis, J. B. eds. Social Capital and Economics. [Online]. London: Routledge, pp. 193–214. [Accessed 26 August 2020]. Available from: https://books.google.co.uk/books?hl=en&lr=&id=6rKuAwAAQBAJ&oi=fnd&pg=PP1&ots=Lx5S6CgWXG&sig=KtNYqJbiacIXoSKHSiIambeuW8w&redir_esc=y#v=onepage&q&f=false

Brennan, G., Tennant, M., and Blomsma, F. 2015. Business and production solutions: closing the loop. In: Kopnina, H., and Shoreman-Ouimet, E. eds. Sustainability: Key Issues. [Online]. London, England, New York, America: EarthScan, Routledge, pp. 219-239. [Accessed 31 August 2020]. Available from: https://books.google.co.uk/books?id=75fwCQAAQBAJ&printsec=frontcover&source=gbs_ge_summary_r&cad=0#v=onepage&q&f=false

Bretos, I., and Marcuello, C. 2017. Revisiting Globalisation Challenges and Opportunities in the Development of Cooperatives. Annals of Public and Cooperative Economics. 88(1), pp. 47-73.

Chertow, M. R. 2000. Industrial symbiosis: literature and taxonomy. Annual Review of Energy and the Environment. 25(1), pp. 313-317.

Dietz, R., O'Neill, D.W., 2013. Enough is enough: building a sustainable economy in a world of finite resources. London: Routledge.

Fernandez-Mena, H., Nesme, T., and Pellerin, S. 2016. Towards an Agro-Industrial Ecology: A review of nutrient flow modelling and assessment tools in agro-food systems at the local scale. Science of the Total Environment. 543(1), pp. 467-479.

Geissdoerfer, M., Savaget, P., Bocken, N. M. P., and Hultink, J. 2017. The Circular Economy – A new sustainability paradigm?. Journal of Cleaner Production. 143(1), pp. 757-768.

Hansmann, H. 1988. Ownership of the firm. Journal of Law, Economics and Organisation. 4(2), pp. 267–304.

Kay, A., Roy, M. J., and Donaldson, C. 2016. Re-imagining social enterprise. Social Enterprise Journal. 12(2), pp. 217-234.

Laamanen, M., Wahlen, S., and Lorek, S. 2018. A moral householding perspective on the sharing economy. Journal of Cleaner Production. 202(1), pp. 1220-1227.

Luzarraga, J. M. 2008. Mondragon Multi–Localisation Strategy: Innovating a Human Centred Globalisation. Ph.D. thesis, University of Mondragon.

Lyle, J. T. Regenerative Design for Sustainable Development. New York, America, Chichester England: John Wiley & Sons.

McDonough, W., and Braungart, M. 2002. Cradle to Cradle: Remaking the Way We Make Things. New York: North Point Press.

McKinsey. 2016. Scaling the impact of the social enterprise sector. [Online]. ed. [no place]: McKinsey & Company. [Accessed 23 August 2020]. Available from: https://www.mckinsey.com/~/media/McKinsey/Industries/Social%20Sector/Our%20Insights/Scaling%20the%20impact%20of%20the%20social%20enterprise%20sector/Scaling-the-impact-of-the-social-enterprise-sector.ashx

Næss, P. 2015. Unsustainable Growth, Unsustainable Capitalism. Journal of Critical Realism. 5(2), pp. 197-227.

OECD. 2019. Boosting Social Entrepreneurship and Social Enterprise Development in the Netherlands, In-depth Policy Review. [Online]. ed. Paris: OECD Publishing. [Accessed 23 August 2020]. Available from: https://www.oecd-ilibrary.org/docserver/4e8501b8-en.pdf?expires=1556013689&id=id&accname=guest&checksum=A14606FE7B272 D03830AF546171488C9&fbclid=IwAR0eIY0MhDgu9tiKiycSoPCop7maa1 ZZgFqIzwDph9INEA4l-BS3H_b8fks

Pearce, J. 2003. Social Enterprise in Anytown. London: Calouste Gulbenkian Foundation.

PwC. 2018. Building an ecosystem for social entrepreneurship: lessons learned from The Netherlands. [Online]. ed. Netherlands: PricewaterhouseCoopers. [Accessed 23 August 2020]. Available from: https://www.pwc.nl/nl/actueel-publicaties/assets/pdfs/pwc-building-an-ecosystem-for-social-entrepreneurship.pdf?fbclid=IwAR3GU4pVj0738ARpKYVBtX8Pfn5384r6cjdTZyggLnTUCBGtW 2SWLKkEn_Q

Rainbow Junk-tion. 2020. Rainbow Junk-tion – the Real Junk Food Project at All Hallows' Café. [Online]. [Accessed 10 September 2020]. Available from: http://rainbowjunktion.org.uk/

Reay, S. D., McCool, J. P., and Withell, A. 2011. Exploring the Feasibility of Cradle to Cradle (Product) Design: Perspectives from New Zealand Scientists. Journal of Sustainable Development. 4(1), pp. 36-44.

Rockström, J., Steffen, W., Noone, K., Persson, A., Chapin III, F. S., Lambin, E., Lenton, T. M., Scheffer, M., Folke, C., Schellnhuber, H., Nykvist, B., De Wit, C. A., Hughes, T., van der Leeuw, S., Rodhe, H., Sorlin, S., Snyder, P. K., Costanza, R., Svedin, U., Falkenmark, M., Karlberg, L., Corell, R. W., Fabry, V. J., Hansen, J., Walker, B., Liverman, D., Richardson, K., Crutzen, P., and Foley, J. A. A safe operating space for humanity. Nature. 461(1), pp. 472-475.

Saavedra, Y. M. B., Iritani, D. R., Pavan, A. L. R., and Ometto, A. R. 2018. Theoretical contribution of industrial ecology to circular economy. Journal of Cleaner Production. 170(1), pp. 1514-1522.

Stahel, W. R. 2016. Circular Economy. Nature. 531(7595), pp. 435-438.

Steffen, W., Richardson, K., Rockstrom, J., Cornell, S., Fetzer, I., Bennett, E., Biggs, R., Carpenter, S., de Vries, W., de Wit, C., Folke, C., Gerten, D., Heinke, J., Mace, G. M., Persson, L M., Ramanathan, V., Reyers, B., and Sörlin, S. 2015. Planetary boundaries: Guiding human development on a changing planet. Science. 347(6223), pp. 736-746.

Stratan, D. 2017. Success Factors of Sustainable Social Enterprises Through Circular Economy Perspectives. Visegrad Journal on Bioeconomy and Sustainable Development. 6(1), pp. 17-23.

Utting, P. 2015. Social and solidarity economy beyond the fringe. London: Zed Books.

Vicari, S. 2014. The cooperative as an institution for human development: the case study of COPPALJ, a primary cooperative in Brazil. Journal of International Development. 26(1), pp. 683-700.

White, R. M., 1979. World Climate Conference: Climate at the Millennium. Environment: Science and Policy for Sustainable Development. 21(3), pp. 31-33.

Wilson, E. 2007. Adapting to Climate Change at the Local Level: The Spatial Planning Response. Local Environment. 11(6), pp. 609-625.

Yune, J. H., Tian, J., Liu, W., Chen, L., and Descamps-Large, C. 2016. Greening Chinese chemical industrial park by implementing industrial ecology strategies: A case study. Resources, Conservation and Recycling. 112(1), pp. 54-64.

Chapter 7

Green Economics Insights - Bringing in Diversity and Inclusion

Miriam Kennet

Introduction

Today, we are probably the richest, most comfortable set of humans who have ever walked the earth, yet we are facing a set of crises as big as any that have ever struck humans in the last 73,000 years – since the Tolba Eruption wiped out half of humanity (Prothero 2018) – and which have the capacity to wipe us out completely, unless we can act together as one humanity in time. The fragility of our survival and well-being, our economy and security is becoming much more evident (Pachauri 2007 in Kennet 2007). The very survival of our species is at risk (Lean 2005 in Kennet 2007). Our economy, the online-knowledge economy, may be the least resilient of any that has gone before, and we are creating health problems for ourselves and other species (IPBES 2019; Wainer, Kennet and Grabauskaite 2015) of unimaginable proportions (Kennet et al. 2012: 33; Watts et al. 2019). NASA (Reddy 2019) has just announced that the arctic soil, which for tens of thousands of years was a carbon sink, has now shifted to becoming a carbon emitter, which will further accelerate the heating of the planet and the rising of sea levels. Patricia Espinosa, Executive Secretary of the United Nations Framework Convention on Climate Change (UNFCCC), recently remarked that our house is on fire. 'If the house is on fire, you don't go back and start negotiating, you do everything possible to put the fire out' (Espinosa 2019). This paper argues that this is possible only if economic policy makers reorientate immediately towards a more realistic, pluralist and holistic interdisciplinary model.

A major part of the problem is our subject of economics, at least the orthodox version, which has been used to justify some of humanity's most destructive acts ever; its ignorance of science, of pluralism and of other disciplines has been instrumental in some of economics' most barbaric and short-sighted policy recommendations and conclusions. The subject is simply not fit for purpose and must undergo transformation and improvement now! This chapter argues that the present climate emergency and coming hostile climate changes, human induced ecological fragility, resource depletion and mass extinction require a specific pluralist, economic science that will offer real and effective change immediately. The mainstream structures are predicated on a 'silo mentality', which has been termed 'monocultures of the mind' (Shiva 1993). An illustration of this point is the theory and practice of monoculture agriculture from the West – a model foisted on the South – that has impoverished farmers. The same can be said of much of mainstream economics. We know that in nature diversity, at all levels, makes a species far more resilient and so a monocultural education, economic discipline and industry, make the world much less resilient and far less able to adapt to the changing dynamic conditions of today. Therefore, in order to achieve a trans formation to a stronger economics discipline, all groups of economists need to 'climb out of their silos' and engage, where appropriate and beneficial, in pluralist method/theory for the purposes of consensual and meaningful policy making. The market can no longer be relied on to deliver or self-regulate, and so crises will continue until it is too late for humanity.

Ban Ki Moon, the previous General Secretary of the United Nations, fam ously declared, 'We are living in an age of Green Economics' (Moon 2008). The current General Secretary António Guterres (*UN News* 2019) has also said 'the Green Economy is the future' (Hermann 2018) and he repeated this in Katowice at COP24 UNFCCC, stating that Green Economics is the 'most important way we can combat climate change' (Guterres 2018). Kennet has always aimed to include natural science data and observations, combined with social science data and narratives, in order to reflect the real world. We build on diverse ideas of ecologism, conservation, socialism, feminism, political economy, counter hegemonism, as well as all aspects of natural science. The ideas are indivisible (not one of them can be simply a social or positivist science), and must now be explored in a holistic manner (Kennet and Heinemann 2006: 3). Kennet and Heinemann argued from the beginning, 'We would fundamentally disagree with departmentalisation economics. We argue for a radical reform of Economics' (Kennet and Heinemann 2006). Harrison (1992) put it well:

It means creating the framework for a more interdisciplinary approach to research and first degrees. The demands of the environment will break down the compartmentalism of knowledge. We desperately need an overarching science of human interactions with the environment combining socio-economic and technical studies with dynamic analysis of the physical environment.(Harrison 1992 in Kennet and Heinemann 2006: 3)

It is imperative to create such a discipline in Green Economics, and it is becoming ever clearer that this methodology is now required by mainstream and pluralist economics in policy and practice. UK Research assessments seemed to move in the other direction, splitting economics into a science concerned solely with mathematics and statistics, removing all other narratives and distancing it from knowledge of geography and the environment from which it receives all its inputs. In our view this policy did untold damage and now needs urgent reversal.

Destructive economic theory, education and policies

The problem has been that economists' graphs with unlabelled axes were allowed to override common sense. It is only when the climate scientists sounded the alarm that the world woke up from their deeply held core belief that the market, and Adam Smith's Invisible Hand, would solve everything and would take care of everyone, that they finally saw what this 'economics plague' had done – the destruction of almost the entire natural world. Today, the race is on to try and stop this process before it is too late, but the toolbox of mainstream economics is not suitable for, or capable of, stopping this destruction. A more holistic set of tools must be brought into use, to reflect the complexity and holism of nature. Green Economics and the Green New Deal, and even the Citizen's Income (Lord 2012), are ideas that have been building support around the world (Kamaruddin and Kennet 2012), and are now taking centre stage. These ideas offer holistic goals based on an economics incorporating much of science, climate science physics, earth science and much more. There are no silos and there are no boundaries, only reality and relevance. This a very different construction of economics based on flourishing, abundance, resilience, survivability and sharing a beautiful world with each other, nature, other species and the planet and its systems (Kennet 2006). Green Economics accepts that human domination is probably not a given and probably won't last. Green Economics is the economics of caring, sharing and supporting each other (Kennet 2019).

Neoclassical economics has always considered the market economy to be able to somehow ensure, as if by magic, that humans make the right decisions, and somehow it will all come out right in the end. But as Stern (2007) stated: 'climate change is the biggest market failure the world has ever seen' and to that failure we could add plastics and dead zones in the sea, air pollution and the sixth largest ever mass extinction of species (Wainer, Kennet and Grabauskaite 2015). Whole seas and lakes are drying up (Marks 2019) whole cities and countries will fall beneath the waves and whole ice sheets are melting (NASA 2019). The North Pole was 35 degrees centigrade warmer in winter 2017 than the average (Watts 2019), and much of the UK and the Netherlands may be underwater in the mid-century.

In spite of the existing environmental stresses, earthquakes are deliberately induced simply by fracking fossil fuels out of the ground. It doesn't take a genius to work out that we are in deep trouble but somehow it seems to have escaped the economists. Their work is almost entirely narrative and qualitative free, future scenario free, long-term free and impact blind. It resides in a silo devoid of human feeling or sensitivity or any kind of ethical enquiry. Its sole aim is to destroy the state to create 'perfect competition' (Friedman 2018) in a world of unspeakable cruelty, combined with a world of deliberate lack of empathy or integrity. The key externality is likely to be simply the destruction of humanity and the entire natural world. To make matters worse, orthodox research has inevitably led to bad education that reproduces the same type of economics and policy for the future. Similarly, a common mainstream tool is to discount the future because (up to now) technology, resources, knowledge and wealth have always increased for humans in historic times. But this is quite possibly about to change. Future generations will be harmed by the economics of this generation and will have fewer resources of all kinds. So, discounting the future when it comes to the economy or the effects of climate change are now being heavily criticised.

In 2008, Queen Elizabeth II famously asked the economists how they managed to entirely fail to predict the Global Financial Crisis (Pierce 2009) – on their own patch – and it may not be surprising that they are not noticing what is going on around them outside of their spreadsheets. It is time to call a halt to this charade. It is time to change what the profession does and how it sees its role. It is time for economists to notice the utter mess they have justified and made. When they have seen the mess, they then need to understand the dynamics and change their methodology and philosophy to lead investment and economies into a more relevant and beneficial outcome. Silo economics has later led to silo education and 'perverse policy incentives' that leave whole economies depending on fossil fuels– this must be reversed. Pluralist economics has some tools available to end this threat to life – but pluralism needs to transform and become more pluralist – aided by holistic insights derived from green economics (Kennet 2014).

The eruption of protest

Many of us involved with pluralist economics are aware of the student led movements that have emerged since the 2008 financial crash, such as the *Manchester Post-Crash Society*, or the international *Rethinking Economics* (also inclusive of lecturers) group. In addition, new institutions like the *Institute for New Economic Thinking* (INET) and *Young Scholars Initiative* (YSI) have also emerged and provide support for the academic economists considering a more pluralist approach. Grassroots protest is also erupting everywhere. Young people, in particular, have had enough and are taking to the streets in utter frustration all over the world in a wave of protests reminis cent of 1848, or even the French Revolution, and they are risking their lives in their thousands from Chile to Hong Kong. At the time of writing this chapter, Hong Kong, Chile, Sweden and many other countries have experienced protests, and this time the young will not be placated or bought off – their very future is what they are trying to defend – and economics appears to have no clear answers. Our Green Economics Institute Television Station, GEIClimateTV, has interviews with young people protesting, showing how they feel disenfranchised and excluded from the economy, and its mainstream actors and institutions (GEITV 2019).

Meanwhile, education today is largely designed to keep people quiet and pacify bystanders, that is, create compliant citizens. In China today, the 'social security system' is tantamount to a citizen subservience points system, and the young people can consume social media but not initiate or even propose anything controversial online – reminiscent of Orwell's 1984. One of the main requests of the climate strikers is that they receive an education fit for their future lives whilst education today is based on a mid-twentieth century discourse where profit and growth were the end game. Today the very same policies, rooted in the mechanics of a failing orthodox mainstream global economic system, are the foundation of the problems we have. Young people need new knowledge, skills and expertise, which is not being provided in schools or universities. And that set of skills and expertise has to reflect the world's phys ical complexity and so it must be pluralist at every level.

The idea that climate change futures can be bought or traded is complete and utter nonsense. Yet, that was the orthodox economist's solution without even mentioning the actual science or physicality of the issues. What we need is for economists to take the lead in showing how an economy will really work in new scenarios, and how people can run their lives today. Given the devastation that Internet shopping causes to the environment or the suicide rates in Amazon or Apple warehouses and factories, the impact of business as usual economics, and the destruction it is causing, needs to be clearly explained to everyone so that they can make much better choices.

So, in order to understand and address these issues, we need to include climate science data on air, water and much more. We need to understand the true impact of economic decision-making, not just as a financial cost– benefit analysis that considers environmental externalities, but one that provides much wider understanding of the impact of our economic system. This naturally involves an interdisciplinary and intradisciplinary work prac tice, delivering professional and workable policies. We have failed as a species and we must reverse the mess.

I lead a delegation to the United Nations Climate Change Convention, the UNFCCC, and as such, the role of economists is to lead, facilitate and enable the response and preparation for stopping climate change and reversing it to ensure the survival of humans, eco-systems and other species. However, economists today appear to be stuck in a time warp of post-Second World War profit, consumption (Rostow 1953) and growth maximisation, massaging income and GDP figures whilst also destroying clean air, water, the sea level, soil and biodiversity and, of course, the climate. It is bizarre, but true, that the short-term rewards are mostly for trashing the planet and other species. Interestingly this week, in the USA, new evidence has emerged that Exon scientists knew about climate change with chilling accuracy 50 years ago and funded and ran a deliberate campaign to deceive the world and to carry on ruining the climate (Hall 2015). They predicted that if they continued their business as usual the climate would warm by about 1 degree centigrade and CO_2 parts per million equivalents would reach 415 – which it has. A video from the Oversight Committee of Congress recorded the evidence and confessions and the actual methods used to deliberately and accurately ruin the world's climate, surely one of the greatest, most far-reaching and damaging crimes humanity has ever committed (Oversight Committee of Congress 2019). The scientists who implemented this campaign of misinformation have confessed and shown everyone the documentary evidence. Thus, they led the precision trashing of the planet in the name of profit and economics. Meanwhile, many people still invest their pension savings in these companies. This means that government regulatory power (including strong sanctions) needs to be enhanced to combat the behaviour of such firms. This requires a stronger political will than has existed hitherto.

The precondition of diversity

If the economics profession is going to be able to achieve a meaningful pluralist approach to its science, then it is helpful for it to be exposed to different voices. I argue in this chapter that, to achieve inter- and/or intradisciplinary work, diversity is a prerequisite. Women's views, for instance, have been absent for much of historic economic thought. In ancient Greece, Aristotle believed that women (half the human species) were too stupid to take part in the economy (Russell 1946: 197). Yet, even today there is a strong chance that if you pick up an economics book, there will be white men on the cover and no women, for example *Modern Macroeconomics* (Snowdon and Vane 2005). Women and their voices are suppressed in a huge number of countries, a ver itable war against women. But do we hear much about this in mainstream economics? Scarcely a peep. It is time to sort this out; both the mainstream and pluralist fields need to become more diverse and inclusive. Different kinds of people inevitably hold 'other' perspectives and the world, the economics and science will be richer for the discourse. In addition, as Plato believed, those who engage more in broader debates are more able to arrive at better decisions and, therefore, make better rulers – or 'philosopher kings', in Plato's termin ology (Russell 1946: 129). However, a key hindrance to the establishment of economic pluralism is that the researchers who engage in broader consider ations are perceived by some to be weaker in their rigour. So, how does the economic profession broaden its discourse, and sources of influence, whilst combatting an economic orthodoxy with a (misguided) superiority complex? Young scholars, for instance, who are keen to establish careers, cannot be expected to be easily incentivised to pursue research programmes deemed to be of limited value and, therefore, non-pluralist practice remains stuck in its own confirmation loop. So, what can be done?

Simply put, economists need to read the newspapers, look at the Internet, link their own work and outcomes to the real world and proactively engage in broader narratives of all descriptions without shame. But, at the same time, also seek to maintain and enhance their academic rigour. Economic policies that directly address the urgent issues of today, and subsequently deliver a measure of beneficial outcomes, will later provide kudos for the economic research on which they are founded. In time truth will emerge into the day light, so contemporary academics are wise to exert more courage. Today we see gangs of people trafficking goods, services and people around the world and the largest migration and slave trade in history (Fielgar and Kennet 2016). The trafficking of women for sweatshops, prostitution or pea-picking in the Mediterranean (for the likes of Tesco) rarely appears in economic models (Tezza and Tezza 2019; Tondo and Kelly 2017). Yet, this is the reality of today. To add to this list of research omissions we can add corrupt regimes, corrupt laws and organised crime spreading on an unimaginable scale. Meanwhile, the general public is losing confidence in government, leaders and experts.

Economics must change now. Pluralist economics has certainly led the profession in the correct direction, but it needs to do more and also provide the tools to deliver this complex change. This chapter argues that a start has been made with green economics, and its sister disciplines and daughters, that is, the green economy, decarbonisation, the green new deal, deep ecology, ecosocialism, the circular economy, and environmental and ecological economics. This Green Economics active commitment to reality, holism and diversity provides a beacon for the pluralist community to follow a sustainable future.

The knowledge economy

Some of the new tools of economic efficiency, and economies of scale, are automation, artificial intelligence and Internet technology. The knowledge economy is predicted to form one-third of the future economy by 2025 – so we ignore it at our peril. Sticking to ordinary graphs and 'business as usual' in economics means to entirely miss the opportunity to devise economic models that account for the forthcoming smart cities and pervasive use of 5G broadband. Is there any meaningful global regulation of it? Absolutely not, so it is no wonder the thieves and criminals are moving in fast and before anyone else. We need a new (knowledge economy) codex and an economic structure which is highly regulated yet still creative and diverse and on a smaller scale (Schumacher 1974), or a medium and regional scale, or global but with appropriately high standards.

The problem with global scale, however, is that, more than ever, IT purchases mean that if we buy parcels from large Internet providers, they rely on larger lorry loads of deliveries using fossil fuels from oppressive regimes, mostly in the Middle East. They destroy whole economies, are subsidised by consumers, and in many countries with huge oil deposits the general populace is deprived of normal income and is far poorer than they should be, for example Albania and Nigeria. But there are alternatives, including locally created renewables, which mitigate the need for global scale, and free up economies to work with less pressure. The future belongs to where large numbers of young people will actually live, especially those with the fastest growing populations, such as Africa or South America. We need to green our purchasing and supply chains (Nutburn 2019), supported properly by mainstream economists.

However, Jeremy Rifkin's powerful vision of an ultra-clean energy renaissance, which some see as the foundation of the German Energiewende Transformation, has already begun a locally derived, interlinked energy democratisation, which offers hope for the sustainability of life on the planet. Crucially, it depends on the development of a smart supergrid that can provide a 'mega-platform' for what Rifkin calls 'the democratisation of energy', a transformation of energy users into producers through the micro-generation of renewable electricity that can be sold back to the grid. (Nelsen 2013) Suggestions for economists, politicians and individuals A pluralist economics, in my view, needs to look at new ways of being physical and practical as it matures more fully, which means spending far more time looking at:

- The long-term considerations – not five- or ten-year business cycle impacts.
- The pre-historic economic conditions prior to the introduction and spread of sedentary lifestyles, agriculture, farming and domestication.
- Temporal and spatial contexts.
- Ancient wisdoms deriving from indigenous peoples.
- How to include everyone, even leaders, in a diverse and inclusive economic model.
- The ecological significance of biodiversity in terms of sustainability.

- The latest scientific predictions of climate change and sea-level rise.
- The multitude of factors impacting global migration.
- Modern supply chain issues, for example, slavery and traffickingThe implication of automation, IT and artificial intelligence.
- Women, gender, inclusion, access and other diversity issues.
- The awareness of changing demographics, for example, the youth of Africa and South America.
- Renewables versus finite resources.
- The development of appropriate economic tools to do all of the above.
- Decolonizing economics and ending the enduring inequalities and lack of economic access caused by casual or violent everyday, state or institu tional racism.

In tandem with this pluralist economics research, and its derived policy, we must also transform the legal system with an inclusive new codex (as far reaching and different as the Hammurabi or Justinian codex, or the Bible) to create a holistic sustainable development. This will serve to regulate the economy in order to make it the servant rather than the master of the people. Here are my recommendations for the political class to pursue in the future:

- We need everyone to monitor their own carbon footprints and cut consumption down.
- We need to end red meat farming and reduce all barbaric livestock management.
- We need to stop using pesticides, fertilisers and hazardous chemicals of all kinds.
- We need to start to value water and ensure we provide free access to it for all the peoples of the earth.
- We need to listen to our human instinct to survive and flourish then build our economics of abundance (Hoeshele 2010) for all species and nature (Kennet 2014; Wainer, Kennet and Grabauskaite 2015).
- We need an end to human trafficking and the arms trade.
- We need to free people from the dependencies of the past, such as oil, debt or slavery.
- We need to outlaw all ethnic cleansing whilst promoting self-determination for peoples.

- We need to support global, national, regional and also local economies, and many other diverse economies such as those of indigenous peoples.
- We need to end the cult of personality and adopt a different kind of leader who has the benefit of all at heart, rather than being drawn to those with more selfish ambitions.

States also need to continue to engage in meaningful and substantive inter national agreement. The Paris COP21 climate conference was enhanced by the fact that all francophone countries carried out the diplomacy. It was they, most importantly, who enabled that historic agreement to happen, as they, and the small island states, are in the frontline of climate change impacts already being felt today and already affecting their economies. I would also advise that everyone becomes familiar with the NASA website that presents us with earth's daily vital signs, such as the number of parts per million CO_2 in the atmosphere, which, at the time of writing, is 412 parts per million, the highest it has been for 600,000 years and an accurate indicator of contemporary warming. Additionally, I would recommend using a carbon checker to reduce our own individual carbon footprint – moving towards 2 tonnes of carbon equivalent consumption per person per year by 2022 and reducing to zero by 2025 (Kennet 2019). To this end, I would suggest the following actions for readers to think about:

- Switch your power source to renewables and switch your transport to work to buses or trains.
- Stop taking cheap short flights for weekend breaks.
- Stop eating too much meat.
- Stop creating all-male platforms and start including women, young/old people and other diversities (Kennet et al. 2012: 33).
- Stop putting pesticides and weed killer in your garden and/or chemicals on your lawns.
- Start supporting politicians/policies that sustain people from 'cradle to grave'.
- Start enabling a future economy and imagining a bright future for humans.
- Start questioning all the supply chains of everything you use.

Conclusion

The simple conclusion is that pluralism is advised to replicate the holistic attributes of green economics, going beyond its past achievements to

120

become fully pluralist, diverse, creative and inclusive – to establish some heterogeneity. The mainstream economists, of course, are welcome to 'join the party'. A reconstructed and holistic economic science can then provide a sustainable basis for a Green Economy (Kennet 2012) or 'a real green new deal' as advocated by *The Guardian* Editorial (*The Guardian* 2019) and in the US Congress House Resolution (No. 109) by Alexandria Ocasia Cortez (in 2019), by fully considering the outcomes from economic policy and evaluating the past. A fundamental barrier to achieving this has been our attachment to the 'silos' of different epistemologies, disciplines, ontologies, theories and methods (Kennet 2009). It is now time to break down the silos and consign them to the dustbin of history before it is too late and before our global economy sinks 'below the waves' forever (Tidman 2019). People now have a brand new enhanced awareness of the present emergency and crises, and a recent understanding of the need to avoid their impossibly colossal costs, that will lead us to find the inclination and courage to work together and cooperate holistically as we, and our species, are designed to do. This will be driven, at least in part, by a new comprehension of the role of, and need for, diversity and togetherness of all peoples everywhere and an economy which nurtures us and our habitat, the earth and its systems and is no longer predicated on its incremental destruction by economic decisions and policy making. Diversity, cooperation and holistic thinking will be the keys to survival as the silos are blown down.

References

Congress House, 2019. *Resolution 109*. Recognizing the duty of the House to create a Green New Deal, Rep. Ocasio-Cortez, Alexandria. Available at: www.congress.gov/bill/116th-congress/house-resolution/109/text, accessed 19 November 2019.

Espinosa, P., 2019. *Our House is on Fire*. Speech to United Nations Research Organisations at the COP24 Katowice, Poland, Climate Conference, December 2018.

Fielgar, H. and Kennet M., 2016. *Introducing Migration, Voices for Social and Environmental Justice*. Reading: The Green Economics Institute.

Friedman, D., 2018. *Oxford Union Debate*, Oxford. Available at: www.youtube.com/ watch?v=Bpn645huKUg, accessed 17 November 2019.

GEITV, 2019. United Nations Climate Change Conference, SB50, Bonn. Interview with Young Climate Protesters. GEIClimateTV. Available at: hiips://vimeo.com/345685818, accessed 19 November 2019.

Guterres, A., 2018. Climate Change and the Need for Green Economics. Speech to the United Nations Climate Change Conference, SB50, June, Bonn, Germany.

GEIClimateTV. Available at: hiips://vimeo.com/308572170, accessed 19 November 2019.

Hall, S., 2015. Exon Knew About Climate Change Almost 40 Years Ago. *Scientific American*, 26 October. Available at: www.scientificamerican.com/article/exxon-knew-about-climate-change-almost-40-years-ago, accessed 19 November 2019.

Hermann, A., 2018. *United Nations Agenda 2030*. Reading: The Green Economics Institute.

Hoeshele, W., 2010. *The Economics of Abundance: A Political Economy of Freedom, Equity, and Sustainability*. Abingdon: Routledge.

IPBES (Intergovernmental Science–Policy Platform for Biodiversity and Ecosystem Services of the United Nations) 2019. *Global Assessment on Biodiversity and Ecosystem Service. Science and Policy for People and Nature*. Available at: hiips://ipbes.net/global-assessment-report-biodiversity-ecosystem-services, accessed 19 November 2019.

Kamaruddin, N. and Kennet M., 2013. *The Greening of Asia and China*. Reading: The Green Economics Institute.

Kennet, M., 2007. Editorial. Background and Rationale for this Next Step in Green Economics. *International Journal of Green Economics*, Vol. 1 (3/4).
Kennet, M., 2009. Green Economics: Emerging Pedagogy in an Emerging Discipline. In J. Reardon, ed., *The Handbook of Pluralist Economics Education*. London and New York: Routledge.

Kennet, M. (ed.) 2012. *The Green Economics Reader*. Reading: The Green Economics Institute.

Kennet, M. ed., 2014. *Rebalancing the Economy*. Reading: The Green Economics Institute.

Kennet, M., 2019. Introduction to Green Economics. What We Do and Why We Do It. Available at: www.greeneconomicsinstitute.org.uk. accessed 19 November 2019.

Kennet, M., Felton J., Gale D'Oliveira, M. and Winchester, A., eds., 2012. Actions for Our Readers in Green Economics. In *Women's Unequal Pay and Poverty*. Reading: Green Economics Institute.

Kennet, M. and Heinemann, V., 2006. Foreword. *International Journal of Green Economics*, Vol. 1 (1/2).

Lord, C., 2012. *Green Economics and a Citizen's Income*, edited by J. Felton. Reading: The Green Economics Institute.

Marks, K., 2019. The World is Running Out of Fresh Water. *Owlcation*, 6 October. Available at: hiips://owlcation.com/stem/10-Worst-Drying-Lakes-in-the-World, accessed 19 November 2019.

Moon, B.K., 2008. *Green Economics speech to the United Nations*. Available at: www. un.org/sg/en/content/sg/articles/2008-10-22/age-green-economics, accessed 19 November 2019.

NASA, 2019. *Global Climate Change, the Vital Signs of the Planet*. Available at: hiips:// climate.nasa.gov/evidence accessed, 19 November 2019.

Nelsen, A., 2013. Jeremy Rifkin Warns Europe: Don't Repeat Obama's Mistakes. *Euractiv*, 21 March. Available at: www.euractiv.com/section/energy/news/jeremy-rifkin-warns-europe-don-t-repeat-obama-s-mistakes, accessed 19 November 2019.

Nutburn, M., 2019. 5 Benefits of a Sustainable Supply Chain. In *Supply Management*. Available at: www.cips.org/en/supply-management/opinion/2019/july/five-benefits-of-a-sustainable-supply-chain, accessed 19 November 2019.

Oversight Committee of Congress, 2019. 'So, They Knew': Ocasio-Cortez Questions Exxon Scientist on Climate Crisis Denial. *The Guardian*, 23 October. Available at:

www.theguardian.com/business/video/2019/oct/23/exxon-alexandria-ocasio-cortez-congress-testimony-climate.

Pierce, A., 2009. The Queen Asks Why No-one Saw the Credit Crunch Coming. *The Telegraph*, 5 November 2008. Available at: www.telegraph.co.uk/news/uknews/theroyalfamily/3386353/The-Queen-asks-why-no-one-saw-the-credit-crunch-coming.html, accessed 19 November 2019.

Prothero, D., 2018. *When Humans Nearly Vanished, The Catastrophic Eruption of Mount Tolba*. New York: Smithsonian Books.

Reddy, S., 2019. Arctic Soil Becomes a Carbon Source Due to Winter Emissions. NASA climate website. Available at: https:// climate.nasa.gov, accessed 19 November 2019.

Rostow, W., 1953. *The Stages of Economic Growth*. Oxford: Wiley, on behalf of the Economic History Society.

Russell, B., 1946. *History of Western Philosophy: And its Connections with Political and Social Circumstances from the Earliest Times to the Present Day*. London: George

Allen and Unwin Ltd. Schumacher, E.F., 1974. Small is Beautiful. In W. Bloom, ed., *Holistic Revolution*, 1st edition. London: Penguin Press.

Shiva, V., 1993. *Monocultures of the Mind, Perspectives on Biodiversity and Biotechnology*. Malaysia: Zed Books.

Snowdon, B. and Vane, H., 2005. *Modern Macroeconomics*. Cheltenham: Edward Elgar. Stern, N., 2007. *The Economics of Climate Change: The Stern Review*. Cambridge: Cambridge University Press.

Tezza, E. and Tezza L., 2019. *Evaluating Corruption: Something Rotten Round the World*. Reading: The Green Economics Institute.

The Guardian, 2019. Editorial. *The Guardian* View of a Green New Deal: We Need It Now. *The Guardian*, May. Available at: www.theguardian.com/commentisfree/2019/may/12/the-guardian-view-on-a-green-new-deal-we-need-it-now, accessed 19 November 2019.

Tidman, Z., 2019. Flood stricken Venice hit by high tide leaving most of the City under water. *The Independent*, 17 November. Available at: www.independent.co.uk/news/world/europe/venice-flooding-70-per-cent-under-water-luigi-brugnaro-a9206361.html, accessed 19 November 2019.

Tondo, L. and Kelly, A., 2017. Raped, Beaten, Exploited: 21st Century Slavery Propping up the Sicilian Economy. *The Guardian*, 12 March. Availableat: www.theguardian.com/global-development/2017/mar/12/slavery-sicily-farming-raped-beaten-exploited-romanian-women, accessed 19 November 2019.

United Nations News, 2019. The Green Economy is the Future. *UN News*, April. Available at: hiips://news.un.org/en/story/2019/04/1037461, accessed 19 November 2019.

Wainer, A., Kennet, M. and Grabauskaite, O., 2015. *Biodiversity Loss, The Variety of Life Under Threat*. Reading: The Green Economics Institute.

Watts, J., 2019. Arctic Warming: Scientists Alarmed by Crazy Temperatures. *The Guardian*, 27 February. Available at: www.theguardian.com/environment/2018/feb/27/arctic-warming-scientists-alarmed-by-crazy-temperature-rises, accessed 19 November 2019.

Watts, N., et al., 2019. The Lancet Countdown on Health and Climate Change: Ensuring that the Health of a Child Born Today is not Defined by a Changing Climate, *The Lancet Countdown*. Vol. 394 (16 November, 10211), pp. 1836–1878.

Part IV
Health and Wellbeing

Chapter 8
Survival solutions and Mental health: the importance of resilience for wellbeing and the role of social prescribing

Dr Alexander Lai and Dr Katherine Kennet

Addressing the Covid-19 pandemic, mental health epidemic, the ensuing effect on wellbeing of the population and healthcare professionals in particular, the benefits of resilience and social prescribing, as well as the links between mental health and climate change.

"Failing to value and invest in mental health during the pandemic risks storing up significant mental and physical health problems for the future – at great human and economic cost."
(The Health Foundation, 2020)

Introduction

There is a growing need as a population to focus on the wellbeing and resilience of individuals and organisations in order to protect from deterioration, burnout and prevent further increases of mental health issues.

Social prescribing provides a novel addition to the current community care. Social prescribing is an add on, not a replacement, to existing care and it provides the opportunity for individuals to connect with their local community and often green spaces in a manner which can be empowering for all involved. In this chapter we will expand on how social prescribing fits into the public's mental health, clinician's wellbeing and how, when used appropriately, there is huge scope for communities to support individual's mental health and wellbeing.

During this unprecedented time of global turmoil it is imperative we learn lessons from the Covid-19 pandemic and the issues it has highlighted within our society that impact our mental and physical wellbeing. We must prepare for the coming onslaught of climate emergencies - mass migration and destabilisation of civilisations which will bring further rises in mental health conditions (Sinclair et al., 2020).

Background

The Covid-19 pandemic has caused a change in daily life on a dramatic scale to people of all ages and in all aspects of society. Since March 23, 2020, when the Government implemented a 'lockdown', people's access to services, right to work and social interactions have been severely limited.
This is not just true of those who contract the virus, but for all members of society asked to change their daily working and personal habits to curb the spread of infections (Joyce and Xu, 2020).

There is a clear risk of a deterioration in mental health for all those affected directly or indirectly by the Covid-19 pandemic and a surge in mental health cases is already being observed at the time of writing - October 2020. In fact mental health services are anticipating an unprecedented "tsunami of delayed mental health impacts" due to the pandemic (Malnick et al., 2020; Holmes et al., 2020).

Social determinants of health are known to be key important factors for an individual's mental and physical health (Marmot et al., 2010). Over the period of austerity [2009-2019] health inequalities have actually worsened rather than improved. As outlined in the 2020 Marmot report: "the most deprived areas and communities [in the UK], particularly in the North of England, have experienced the greatest declines in funding in almost all social, economic and cultural domains, and poverty, poor health and socioeconomic inequalities have increased" (Marmot et al., 2020). This has resulted in a very unequal landscape pre-pandemic, and factors such as age, sex, race and socioeconomic status, are likely to continue to be crucial determinants for all aspects of individual's health, both mental and physical, as the pandemic continues. In fact, it would be unsurprising if this inequality in health outcomes didn't become an even more pronounced factor (McManus et al., 2019).

The pandemic and measures to combat it, such as 'lockdown' and reduced social contact, have had devastating implications for those in society who were already experiencing significant socioeconomic burden. Examples include those on zero-hour contracts, single-parent or multi-member households and housing instability. This has contributed to increases in cases of domestic violence, loss of income and loss of structured social interactions. It is therefore easy to understand how when faced with such significant life stressors those individuals' mental health have suffered as a consequence, and, in turn, how this mental health strain on society has been unequal in its distribution (Andrew et al., 2020; Benzeval et al., 2020).

Other more personal factors have played a part in determining the impact the Covid-19 pandemic has had on an individual's mental health. Personality, genetics, past history or mental health issues as well as the social factors already mentioned, all have an impact on an individual's risk. Furthermore changes in peoples' daily routines including the loss of a commute, change to school and work activities and amount of time spent with household members have all contributed to an alteration in mental health and this has not been entirely negative (Townsend, 2020).Anxieties about infection risk have caused undue stress for those with a predisposition to health anxiety, however for younger adolescents who struggle with exam fears, reduced school stress has been found to result in less anxiety and better mental health (Royal College of Psychiatrists 2020 Annual National Child and Adolescent Conference, 2020).

At the time of writing - October 2020, the pandemic has a long way to go before the physical health impact is fully known, let alone the mental health impacts. However, at this early stage, we have already seen evidence of groups adversely affected, for example, in the UK older adolescent females, a group who have already been increasingly presenting to mental health services with acts and thoughts of suicide and self harm, are expeiecning an increase in the rate of these presentations. A study from April 2020 based in America which compared rates of psychological distress in adults found a similar trend with the greatest increase in distress in women, and in the 18-24 age group (McGinty et al., 2020).

Research such as this which identifies those who are most vulnerable to impacts on their mental health from the pandemic, is crucial to managing the ensuing rise in mental health issues.

Wellbeing, Employment and Resilience

Wellbeing

The World Health Organisation defines 'Health' as "a state of complete physical, mental and social wellbeing and not merely the absence of disease or infirmity" (WHO, 2020).

However to truly define 'Wellbeing' from a holistic and less descartian separation of mind and body, we need to incorporate the broader concepts of resilience for overall life happiness, including: autonomy, connection, satisfaction, and purpose. With this in mind, the New Economics Foundation describes wellbeing as the following:

"Wellbeing can be understood as how people feel and how they function, both on a personal and a social level, and how they evaluate their lives as a whole" (2012).

Maintaining stable wellbeing relies on individuals having the psychological, social and physical resources they need to meet a particular psychological, social and/or physical challenge. Common psychological, social and physical resources include mindfulness, a positive mindset, having meaningful interactions with family and friends, eating a healthy diet and exercise.

Wellbeing and Covid-19

In addition to presenting new or enhanced stressors, Covid-19 has had multiple direct and indirect consequences that diminish these resources used to cope with stress. These include, but are not limited to:

- Loss of financial security, income or employment that can have a profound effect on wellbeing. These issues extend beyond the financial benefits including loss of purpose, routine and social network. The Mental Health Foundation reports "over a third of people in full-time work surveyed were concerned about losing their job" (2020).
- Conflicting messages from authorities and media and general uncertainty leading to feelings of lack of control and heightened anxiety.
- Physical illness and mortality, of both your own and your loved ones. Loss of someone during isolation has a profound effect on

your mental and physical health, as does severe illness or anxiety around the illness.

- Restrictions, leading to loss of human interaction, social connectedness, ability to exercise and personal autonomy.

There are of course inequalities in these deficits: "job loss is socioeconomically patterned, some groups cannot get outdoors, and some are unable to remain digitally connected to friends and family" (The Health Foundation, 2020). All of this raises the risk that mental health and wellbeing gaps will escalate with the pandemic.

The Lockdown Paradox

A minority of individuals may have experienced an increase in mental wellbeing following Covid-19. There is evidence to suggest people develop improved coping strategies following major disasters, for example there was a reduced number of mental health presentations following the events of September 11th 2001 (Bonanno et al., 2006). This belies the concept of resilience whereby people develop strategies that enable them to better manage their wellbeing when faced with further adversity. Some reasons for this improvement in wellbeing may include increased contact with a support network, with larger units living at home with family or a preference for working from home.

With enforced lockdowns across the globe and fear about health issues, we witnessed members of the public develop an appreciation for their life pre-Covid-19 and a subsequent focus on prioritising health and social interaction, with a rise in people proactively engaging in activities to improve their wellbeing. Popular methods included connecting with their local communities, taking up new hobbies or learning new skills and increased communication with family and friends digitally.
Furthermore there was an increase in the number of people trying to improve their physical wellbeing by beginning exercise regimes to make use of the Government sanctioned '1 hour exercise window' and the complimentary public exercise products available. These activities included online video gym and yoga sessions, a large increase in the number of people running or jogging outdoors, utilisation of local and national parks and a massive uptake in cycling which was supported with government subsidies. Combined we observed a rise in social connection with more families engaging in activities outdoors. With the pandemic still continuing into the winter of 2020 in the UK, it remains to be seen whether these new wellbeing habits will be sustained.

Wellbeing and work

For businesses, having happy, healthy staff is of course crucial, albeit not always prioritised.

Cooper et al. (2010) noted that there are a number of key issues facing organisations as a result of mental health and wellbeing issues:

- Costs of depleted mental health to England as a whole are estimated to be £77 billion per annum
- Stress and a lack of wellbeing in the work are estimated to amount to £25.9 billion per annum. in the UK. This is a result of sickness absence, presenteeism and labour turnover.

Economic reasons aside there is a plethora of evidence that happy, motivated staff are more productive and lead to better customer satisfaction, lower staff turnover and easier recruitment.

Furthermore for the individual, there are numerous benefits to having a job than just the apparent financial incentives. Being employed can give an individual a sense of purpose, a reason to get out of bed in the morning and a routine. Work can also foster new social relationships providing individuals with the opportunity to connect with others. These interactions with colleagues also result in a variety of factors that have a positive impact on wellbeing including building trust, confidence and social support (Bradbury and Lichenstein, 2000).

Employment can also provide a sense of achievement through acknowledgement of skills and competence and studies show an association "between various psychosocial characteristics of work, including job satisfaction, job demands/control, effort/reward, and various subjective measures of general health and psychological wellbeing" (Waddel and Burton 2006).

While work can have a positive impact on wellbeing, unprecedented events such as this pandemic and its consequences can obviously have a negative impact on our wellbeing at work leading to burnout and subsequent exhaustion. Burnout is "the result of chronic workplace stress that has not been successfully dealt with and is characterised by overwhelming exhaustion, a sense of cynicism and detachment from work" (Maslach, Schaufeli and Leiter, 2001). Research suggests that burnout is a strong predictor of depression (Shin et al. 2013).

Wellbeing in healthcare professionals

Unsurprisingly given their key role in managing the pandemic, there has been a significant deterioration in their wellbeing and a subsequent rise in rates of burnout amongst healthcare professionals. With NHS staff having to drastically change their ways of working there was a significant burden placed on them with ensuing mental health issues. Research found the key predictors to be "working long hours, lack of support and vital equipment, feelings of vulnerability or loss of control, concerns about health of oneself and one's family and feeling isolated" (Kinman et al., 2020).

Further factors included working in unfamiliar environments, constantly changing protocols and exposure to death and trauma without appropriate training or opportunity for feedback. This was all compounded by conflicting emotions of guilt, ethical and moral obligation that challenged personal routines of self care.

Hospital staff were noted to be exhibiting various signs of mental distress including irritability and an unwillingness to rest as well as a refusal to engage with psychological approaches. Multiple healthcare professionals went off sick or approached their GP for help having burnt out and sadly some committed suicide.

All of this is of grave concern, especially given pre-Covid-19 reviews of the healthcare workforce had already found high rates of demoralisation, stress and burnout in part as a result of increased demands and a reduction in staffing levels and other resources (Kinman et al., 2020).

In order to tackle these issues, many professional bodies prioritised health and wellbeing of healthcare staff and there was a sudden and welcome upsurge in evidence-informed support initiatives to mitigate these effects on their current and future wellbeing. An array of resources were collated and created such as national text messaging services and helplines, free counselling, cognitive behavioural therapy and access to online tools and webinars

Organisations such as The Workwell Doctors ran free 'Resilience & Wellbeing' workshops for healthcare professionals to help them identify the early signs of stress and burnout, manage the higher rates of anxiety, grief, uncertainty and insomnia and ensure they prioritized self-care to mitigate work and life stressors.

Resilience

Resilience is often defined as 'bouncing back' from a difficult situation (Ackerman, 2020). So a person with high levels of resilience should, in theory, be more capable of handling difficult situations in comparison to someone with low levels of resilience.
There are three issues with this definition:

- It assumes you have to have adversity to learn from it. We can all build our resilience by learning from others' suffering and what actions they took to recover.

-

- It assumes that resilience can only be built afterwards whereas the key point is to learn how to recognise challenges, set up strategies in advance, and engage these steps before reaching burnout.

-

- It's not about bouncing back to where you were before, it's about growing from each setback and being further ahead each time you face a challenge.

Resilience training is not just something to engage in during recovery but should be initiated throughout our lives to improve our wellbeing, thereby making us more prepared for inevitable challenges to come. Research on resilience originated from studies of adults who had survived childhood trauma (Bonanno, 2004) and there is now a host of bodies studying the beneficial effects of incorporating resilience training for children in schools to cope (Sapienzza, 2011).

Focussing on personal resilience should be a priority not something left until we have enough time and is increasingly vital for future generations' wellbeing as they deal with evolving geo-political, technological and ecological issues.

We recognise that resilience training is no substitute for addressing issues in the workplace and system. Resilience training is a 'secondary prevention measure', changing the system and workplace is primary prevention and therefore potentially more impactful, but may not be fully in our control. Also resilience is contextual, we are all resilient with what we are used to dealing with, it's the unexpected challenges that can exert extra pressure. However we can be better prepared to protect us from the inevitable further insults to our wellbeing.

Resilient people are often noted to have a certain mindset with several common characteristics, all of which can be learnt. There is a wealth of research that shows you can influence how you think and respond in ways that help you to navigate tough times. The key strategies can be categorised under the following attributes:

Purpose

This begins with determining your values i.e. what matters to you most or what drives you, in order to establish a reason to keep going. It is characterised by a strong sense of self-worth which influences what direction to pursue in life. By being aware of the destination, experiencing 'bumps in the road' are seen as only part of the longer term journey - thereby minimising any short term stressors. Also by living by a set of values, deciding what tasks in work or life to take on becomes easier, thereby creating a set of boundaries to reduce the risk of becoming overburdened or burnt out.

Tenacity

Things will always go wrong, resilient people recognise this and have a willingness to keep going. Being persistent is more important than intelligence in working towards a goal. By having a realistic sense of optimism and hopefulness about the future, challenges become easier to overcome. An understanding that suffering is a part of life means that when things go wrong, there is also less likelihood of feeling persecuted.

Perspective

This is about understanding our own emotions, recognising them and questioning if getting upset or stressed about a situation is actually a benefit or detriment to ourselves. It is also important to ask ourselves whether there is another side to the situation, thereby increasing our compassion and helping us to better understand and accept a difficult situation.

Resourcefulness

This is achieved through critical thinking, anticipating things going wrong, doing things ahead of time and learning from others. Taking proactive actions can help minimise disruption in the future.

Embracing Change

As humans we are evolutionarily developed to recognise threats and weaknesses to protect ourselves. Resilient people don't diminish the negative but have found ways to focus on the positives in situations.

Change is ever-present: developing the ability to find opportunity in change is vital. Focus is directed towards issues within our control that can be changed or influenced, as well as acceptance of the things we can not.

Community

Having supportive networks and meaningful connections is imperative to our resilience. Developing relationships so that we have people there when things get tough can have a huge impact on our wellbeing. Conversely, being there to support others through their own challenges can be fulfilling and acts of kindness are proven to improve wellbeing. It can take time to build these relationships and therefore proactiveness and the willingness to invest time are important.

Healthiness

Resilience is more than just a mindset, it includes all the aspects that encompass physical health such as good nutrition, adequate sleep and exercise. A healthy body enables effective crisis response and gives a better chance of surviving any health emergencies. Furthermore not caring for your mind and body can lead to a disruption later in life.
(The Resilient Doc, 2020)

Through appropriate training and adoption of these attributes we hope that the current population and future generations will become more resilient and thus better prepared to withstand the onslaught of further assaults to their wellbeing.

Social prescribing

Social prescribing is the term for individuals being put in touch with groups and programs in their local community to support their health and wellbeing. It sits alongside more traditional treatments for mental and physical illness, such as medication and talking therapies. Social prescribing can be of benefit to all people with all manner of health difficulties.

Social prescribing in the UK most commonly uses the link worker model, where an individual either refers themselves, or is referred by their GP, another clinician or teacher, to a link worker. Link workers are not medically trained, but work in specific communities and are aware of all community groups and third sector organisations running in the local area. A link worker will be skilled at listening to the individuals they work with and meet with them for a one-off consultation where they ask the question "what matters to you?". By exploring the individual's interests and health needs, the Link worker will signpost the individual to community groups which meet their needs and match their interests.

Social prescribing groups can be hugely diverse and are not condition specific. Someone with a diagnosis of diabetes or high blood pressure may benefit from an exercise group, a cooking or food growing group, but they may find a creative skills based group such as pottery may help their self esteem, confidence, loneliness or low mood. Physical and mental health disorders are often intrinsically linked: in the UK 30% of the population live with one or more long term physical health conditions, of which 26% also have a mental health problem (Naylor et al, 2012). An example of this is that, in the UK, people with cancer, diabetes, asthma and high blood pressure are at greater risk of a range of mental health problems such as depression, anxiety and PTSD (Mental health statistics: physical health conditions, 2020). Addressing the mental or physical health issues of one can only have positive effects on the other.

The community groups on offer in any given area will be dependent on local availability, and what has organically evolved over time; rural areas will have very different groups to those in urban areas. When social prescribing is working well, the groups will nourish the communities in which they sit, and those attending will often become group leaders over time. For the individuals attending groups there should always be true autonomy in terms of choosing to attend. In mental health care in particular, for those with a severe and enduring mental illness, there is frequently a sense of being done "to" rather than "with", and good social prescribing can enable individuals to feel they have power and autonomy over at least one part of their recovery.

Social prescribing is not just for individuals who are acutely unwell. It can be hugely beneficial for those who are recovering, in remission from a disorder, living with a chronic physical or mental illness and for prevention of illness. Individuals may benefit from different groups at different stages of their illness journey.

Social prescribing often features the natural world, and enables individuals and communities to reap the benefits of being in and connecting to nature. There is evidence that mental health disorders affecting people of all ages can experience improvement of symptoms from being in nature. For example children with attention deficit hyperactivity disorder (ADHD) have reduced symptoms when exposed to activities in outdoor settings (Kuo and Faber Taylor, 2004). Furthermore people with depression experienced improved mood and cognitive ability after 50 minutes in an arboretum (Berman et al., 2012) and improved symptoms were noted in those with

137

Alzeimers disease when animal assisted therapy was used (Cevizci, Murat Sen, Gunes and Karaahmet, 2020).

The helpful effect of nature to mental and physical health is clear in evidence from acute stress, (Van Den Berg and Custers, 2010) overall mental wellbeing (Wheeler, White, Stahl-Timmins and Depledge, 2012) to the severe and enduring mental illnesses such as schizophrenia (Holley, 2011). We have seen during the Covis-19 lockdowns, when the opportunity to interact with our immediate natural surroundings was limited or for some completely taken away, how much we miss nature. One of the silver linings of the Covid-19 lockdowns was this appreciation of nature and social prescribing offers a chance for people of all ages and in all geographical locations to connect with nature; green walks in even the most urbanised areas can be of benefit. The lockdowns have also highlighted the importance of social connectedness, and the importance of social contact, even if this is socially distanced or virtual.
The World Health Organisation has advised that for older adults, particularly those with dementia or those living alone, the periods of quarantine and social isolation can lead to higher levels of agitation, stress, anger and anxiety. They have highlighted the importance of families and communities as well as health professionals in providing emotional and practical support during this period (WHO, 2020). Social prescribing provides these connections between individuals and their community.

Social prescribing when managed well is a highly sustainable addition to health and wellbeing services. It enables people to interact with their community, build community links and connect with nature. It should never however be seen as a cheap alternative to medical, psychological or social care. For social prescribing to thrive, the community must be adequately supported. Sustainable healthcare should encompass these core principles:

c   Prioritise prevention
d   High value care
e   Empowering individuals and their communities
f   Empower staff
g   Reduce waste and consider carbon (RCPsych, 2020)

Clearly social prescribing, when done in a manner that is sensitive to communities, meets these criteria and can therefore be described as truly sustainable. It is therefore an important step towards the NHS' goal of reaching net zero carbon by 2050 (For a greener NHS » A Net Zero NHS, 2020). The most sustainable health outcome is prevention and keeping patients well as this does not require the human, financial and carbon cost of inpatient stays and significantly increased resource input.

There is evidence that social prescribing improves emotional and psychological wellbeing, improves quality of life, increases confidence and self esteem, reduces social isolation, reduces loneliness, improves physical health and reduces levels of anxiety and depression, (Chatterjee et al., 2017) which makes this a truly sustainable health intervention (Chatterjee, 2018).

Mental health and climate change

This global pandemic has been a crucial example of how devastating world events can cause a worsening of health and health inequalities. It is vital that the current increase in mental health disorders is seen in the context of the national and global social changes.

Mental health issues were on the rise prior to Covid-19, however during this pandemic, this trend has worsened. By ensuring we have a sustainable, well resourced and resilient mental and physical health service we are preparing our health system for the oncoming mental health tidal wave due to Covid-19.
We are also ensuring a resilient workforce and health system which can continue to care for those who are already unwell and those who will be in dire need as a result of oncoming inevitable challenges, such as the impending post pandemic recession and escalating climate and ecological emergency.

The impacts of the climate and ecological emergency on mental health are enormous. Some impacts are immediate such as heat waves, or short term such as tornadoes and floods, or long term such as prolonged drought, deforestation and forced migration. All these drastic events can affect the mental health of a population, with the developments of disorders such as post-traumatic stress disorder (PTSD), increased substance misuse, depression and eco-distress (Cianconi et al., 2020). Eco-distress, also called eco-anxiety, is where individuals, often young people, feel anger, anxiety and apathy when faced with the current planetary crisis, particularly seeing an inadequate response by those in positions of power. Although not a mental health disorder itself, the subsequent feelings of hopelessness and despair over loss can be clinically significant, and cause severe distress and mental health issues for individuals (Pihkala, 2018).

Natural disasters, once seen as freak events, are increasing in frequency (Republic World, 2020) as the climate emergency accelerates, and are causing PTSD and the well known poor mental health effects of migration. (Parker et al., 2020)

With regards to natural disasters within the UK, the prevalence of mental health symptoms including depression, anxiety and psychological distress were found to be two to five times higher in those who had been flooded than those who had not (Siriwardhana, 2013).

Migration, often caused by natural disasters and changing habitats, leads to a forced change in living areas. This carries with it the increased risk of severe and enduring mental illness such as schizophrenia, the risk of xeno-phobia in the host country and subsequent distress for all involved (Siri-wardhana and Stewart, 2013; Gleick, 2014).

In addition to causing mental health issues, climate change also has a sig-nificant impact on those with a preexisting mental health issue: those who have a mental health disorder are three times more likely to die secondary to a heat wave than those who do not have a mental health diagnosis. There is also a clear association between suicide rates in early summer and warm-ing temperatures and there is evidence of a clear link between air pollution and dementia (Gleick, 2014).

Consequences of climate change, such as the economic and social difficulty, affect vulnerable populations and contribute not only to the increase in the incidence of mental illnesses in the affected population but also in sub-sequent generations (Cianconi, 2020).

During the Covid-19 pandemic it has become evident that certain groups of people are more vulnerable during systemic pressures on mental health than others. These vulnerable individuals who have been at higher risk to Covid-19 such as those with pre-existing mental or physical health condi-tions, the elderly, those in poor socio-economic situations, those with intel-lectual disabilities and countless others, will also be most likely at higher risk from the health threats that the climate and ecological emergency brings. It is essential for us to learn from the Covid-19 pandemic and en-sure the more vulnerable members of society have the health and social systems in place to support them.

Conclusion

It is evident that the Covid-19 pandemic has caused a further increase on the already rising trend in mental health morbidity over recent years. It is imperative that we act now to protect the wellbeing of our healthcare workers and systems in order to provide sustainable healthcare in the future.

It is important that social prescribing and resilience building are not simply used as an excuse not to provide safe working conditions or easily accessible holistic health care. It should be provided by a cohesive team of diversely skilled professionals from a range of disciplines who have the time, appropriate funding and support to explore the medical and social determinants of health that affect our physical and mental wellbeing.

The authors strongly advocate for resilience training and social prescribing to be appropriately incorporated into society to prepare for the impending pandemic of mental health issues caused not just by the Covid-19 pandemic but also the climate and ecological emergencies which are rapidly escalating. These tools are one of many survival solutions which when integrated will ensure we have a resilient healthcare workforce and system to not just manage the illness in our society, but that can help it thrive sustainably for years to come.

References

Ackerman, C., 2020. What Is Resilience And Why Is It Important To Bounce Back?. [online] PositivePsychology.com. Available at: <https://positivepsychology.com/what-is-resilience/> [Accessed 4 October 2020].

Andrew, A., Sevilla, A., Phimister, A., Krutikova, S., Kraftman, L., Farquharson, C., Costa Dias, M., Cattan, S., 2020. How are mothers and fathers balancing work and family under lockdown?

Arnold, J., Randall, R. 2016. Work Psychology: Understanding Human Behaviour in the Workplace. Harlow, England: Pearson.

Benzeval, M., Read, B., Low, H., Jäckle, A., Fisher, P., Crossley, T. and Burton, J., 2020. The idiosyncratic impact of an aggregate shock: the distributional consequences of COVID-19.

Berman, M., Kross, E., Krpan, K., Askren, M., Burson, A., Deldin, P., Kaplan, S., Sherdell, L., Gotlib, I. and Jonides, J., 2012. Interacting with nature improves cognition and affect for individuals with depression. Journal of Affective Disorders, 140(3), pp.300-305.

Bonanno, G., Galea, S., Bucciarelli, A. and Vlahov, D. 2006. Psychological Resilience After Disaster. Psychological Science, 17(3), pp.181-186.

Bonanno, G., Diminich, E.D. 2004. Annual research review: Positive adjustment to adversity – trajectories of minimal-impact resilience and emergent resilience. J Child Psychol Psychiatry. 2012; 54(4): 378-401. Am Psychol. 2004; 59(1): 20-28.

Bradbury, H., Bergmann Lichtenstein, B. M. 2000. 'Relationality in Organizational Research: Exploring the Space Between'. Organization Science, 11 (5), 551-564.

Cevizci, S., Murat Sen, H., Gunes, F. and Karaahmet, E., 2020. Animal Assisted Therapy And Activities In Alzheimer's Disease. [online] Cdn.intechopen.com. Available at: <http://cdn.intechopen.com/pdfs-wm/43126.pdf> [Accessed 18 October 2020].

Chatterjee, H., Camic, P., Lockyer, B. and Thomson, L., 2017. Non-clinical community interventions: a systematised review of social prescribing schemes. Arts & Health, 10(2), pp.97-123.

Cianconi, P., Betrò, S. and Janiri, L. 2020. The Impact of Climate Change on Mental Health: A Systematic Descriptive Review. Frontiers in Psychiatry, 11.

Cooper, C.L. 2010. 'Mental Capital and Well-being'. Stress and Health [online] 26 (1), 1-2. Available at: <https://locate.coventry.ac.uk/primo-explore/fulldisplay?docid=TN_scopus2-s2.0-75849150189&context=PC&vid=COV_VU1&search_scope=Primo_Central&tab=remote&lang=en_US> [Accessed 13 October 2020].

Crd.york.ac.uk. 2020. The Effects Of Physical Activity On Psychological Well-Being For Those With Schizophrenia: A Systematic Review. [online] Available at: <https://www.crd.york.ac.uk/crdweb/ShowRecord.asp?ID=12011004466&ID=12011004466> [Accessed 18 October 2020].

Dodge, R., Daly, A.P., Huyton, J., Sanders, L.D. 2012. 'The Challenge of Defining Wellbeing' International Journal of Wellbeing [online] 2 (3), 222-235. Available at: https://internationaljournalofwellbeing.org/index.php/ijow/article/view/89 [Accessed 12 October 2020].

England.nhs.uk. 2020. For A Greener NHS » A Net Zero NHS. [online] Available at: <https://www.england.nhs.uk/greenernhs/a-net-zero-nhs/> [Accessed 18 October 2020].

Holley, J., Crone, D., Tyson, P. and Lovell, G., 2011. The effects of physical activity on psychological well-being for those with schizophrenia: A systematic review. British Journal of Clinical Psychology, 50(1), pp.84-105.

Holmes, E., O'Connor, R., Perry, V., Tracey, I., Wessely, S., Arseneault, L., Ballard, C., Christensen, H., Cohen Silver, R., Everall, I., Ford, T., John, A., Kabir, T., King, K., Madan, I., Michie, S., Przybylski, A., Shafran, R., Sweeney, A., Worthman, C., Yardley, L., Cowan, K., Cope, C., Hotopf, M. and Bullmore, E., 2020. Multidisciplinary research priorities for the COVID-19 pandemic: a call for action for mental health science. The Lancet Psychiatry, 7(6), pp.547-560.

Joyce, R., Xu, X., 2020. Sector shutdowns during the coronavirus crisis: which workers are most exposed? IFS Briefing Note. The Institute for Fiscal Studies. [online] Available at: <https://www.ifs.org.uk/publications/14791> [Accessed 13 October 2020].

Kinman, G., Teoh, K. and Harriss, A., 2020. Supporting the well-being of healthcare workers during and after COVID-19. Occupational Medicine, 70(5), pp.294-296.

Kuo, F. and Faber Taylor, A., 2004. A Potential Natural Treatment for Attention-Deficit/Hyperactivity Disorder: Evidence From a National Study. American Journal of Public Health, 94(9), pp.1580-1586.

Gleick, P., 2014. Water, Drought, Climate Change, and Conflict in Syria. Weather, Climate, and Society, 6(3), pp.331-340.

Malnick, E., Bird, S., Penna, D., Mendick, R., 2020. Coronavirus Will Cause Global 'Tsunami' Of Mental Health Problems Worse Than 2008 Financial Crash, Harvard Warns. [online] The Telegraph. Available at: <https://www.telegraph.co.uk/news/2020/09/26/coronavirus-will-cause-global-tsunami-mental-health-problems/> [Accessed 17 October 2020].

Marmot, M., Goldblatt, P., Allen, J., 2010. Fair Society Healthy Lives (The Marmot Review). [online] Institute of Health Equity. Available at: <http://www.instituteofhealthequity.org/resources-reports/fair-society-healthy-lives-the-marmot-review> [Accessed 17 October 2020].

Marmot, M., Allen, J., Boyce, T., Goldblatt, P., Morrison, J., 2020. Health Equity in England: The Marmot Review ten years on. London: [online] Institute of Health Equity. Available at: <http://www.instituteofhealthequity.org/resources-reports/marmot-review-10-years-on/the-marmot-review-10-years-on-executive-summary.pdf> [Accessed 17 October 2020].

Mental Health Foundation. 2020. Mental Health Statistics: Physical Health Conditions. [online] Available at: <https://www.mentalhealth.org.uk/statistics/mental-health-statistics-physical-health-conditions> [Accessed 18 October 2020].

Maslach, C., Schaufeli, W. and Leiter, M., 2001. Job Burnout. Annual Review of Psychology, 52(1), pp.397-422.

McGinty, E., Presskreischer, R., Han, H. and Barry, C., 2020. Psychological Distress and Loneliness Reported by US Adults in 2018 and April 2020. JAMA, 324(1), p.93.

McManus, S., Bebbington, P., Jenkins, R., Morgan, Z., Brown, L., Collinson, D., Brugha, T., 2019. Data Resource Profile: Adult Psychiatric Morbidity Survey (APMS). International Journal of Epidemiology, 49(2), pp.361-362e.

Naylor, C., Parsonage, P., McDaid, D., Knapp, M., Fossey, M., Galea, A., 2012. Long-term conditions and mental health: The cost of co-morbidities. Kingsfund.org.uk. [online] Available at: <https://www.kingsfund.org.uk/sites/files/kf/field/field_publication_file/long-term-conditions-mental-health-cost-comorbidities-naylor-feb12.pdf> [Accessed 13 October 2020].

New Economics Foundation. 2012. Measuring Wellbeing: A guide for practitioners, London: New Economics Foundation.

Parker, G., Lie, D., Siskind, D., Martin-Khan, M., Raphael, B., Crompton, D. and Kisely, S., 2020. Mental Health Implications For Older Adults After Natural Disasters – A Systematic Review And Meta-Analysis.

Pfefferbaum, B. and North, C., 2020. Mental Health and the Covid-19 Pandemic. New England Journal of Medicine, [online] 383(6), pp.510-512. Available at: <https://www.nejm.org/doi/full/10.1056/NEJMp2008017> [Accessed 12 October 2020].

Pihkala, P., 2018. ECO-ANXIETY, TRAGEDY, AND HOPE: PSYCHOLOGICAL AND SPIRITUAL DIMENSIONS OF CLIMATE CHANGE. Zygon®, 53(2), pp.545-569.

Rcpsych.ac.uk. 2020. How To Be A Sustainable Psychiatrist. [online] Available at: <https://www.rcpsych.ac.uk/docs/default-source/improving-care/sustainability/sustainability-day-top-ten-tips.pdf?sfvrsn=fcc6b3d6_4> [Accessed 13 October 2020].

Republic World. 2020. UN: Climate Change Has Led To The Doubling Of Natural Disasters Since 2000 - Republic World. [online] Available at: <https://www.republicworld.com/world-news/rest-of-the-world-news/climate-change-leads-to-a-doubling-in-natural-disasters-since-2000.html> [Accessed 13 October 2020].

Sapienza, J., Masten, A. 2011. Understanding and promoting resilience in children and youth. Curr Opin Psychiatry;24:267-273.

Shin, H., Noh, H., Jang, Y., Park, Y., Lee, S. 2013. 'A longitudinal examination of the relationship between teacher burnout and depression'. Journal of Employment Counseling [online] 50 (3), 124-137.

Sinclair, C., O'Shea, N., Allwood, L. and Durcan, G.. 2020. At Least Half A Million More People In UK May Experience Mental Ill Health As A Result Of Covid-19, Says First Forecast From Centre For Mental Health | Centre For Mental Health. [online] Available at: <https://www.centreformental-health.org.uk/news/least-half-million-more-people-uk-may-experience-mental-ill-health-result-covid-19-says-first-forecast-centre-mental-health> [Accessed 13 October 2020].

Siriwardhana, C. and Stewart, R., 2012. Forced migration and mental health: prolonged internal displacement, return migration and resilience. International Health, 5(1), pp.19-23.

The Health Foundation. 2020. Emerging Evidence On COVID-19'S Impact On Mental Health And Health Inequalities | The Health Foundation. [online] Available at: <https://www.health.org.uk/news-and-comment/blogs/emerging-evidence-on-covid-19s-impact-on-mental-health-and-health> [Accessed 13 October 2020].

The Resilient Doc. 2020. Resilience & Wellbeing Training <www.theresilientdoc.com> <https://www.instagram.com/the_resilient_doc/> [online] [Accessed 13 October 2020].

Townsend, E., Nielsen, E., Allister, R. and Cassidy, S., 2020. Key ethical questions for research during the COVID-19 pandemic. The Lancet Psychiatry, 7(5), pp.381-383.

Van Den Berg, A. and Custers, M., 2010. Gardening Promotes Neuroendocrine and Affective Restoration from Stress. Journal of Health Psychology, 16(1), pp.3-11.

Waddell, G., Burton, A. K. (2006) Is Work Good for Your Health and Wellbeing? An Independent Review [online] available from https://www.gov.uk/government/publications/is-work-good-for-your-health-and-well-being [10th May 2019]

Wheeler, B., White, M., Stahl-Timmins, W. and Depledge, M., 2012. Does living by the coast improve health and wellbeing?. Health & Place, 18(5), pp.1198-1201.

Who.int. 2020. World Health Organisation. [online] Available at: <https://www.who.int/docs/default-source/coronaviruse/mental-health-considerations.pdf?sfvrsn=6d3578af_22020> [Accessed 18 October 2020].

World Health Organization 2020. Constitution. [online] Available at: <https://www.who.int/about/who-we-are/constitution> [Accessed 12 October 2020].

Part V
Corruption and Institutions

Chapter 9

Combating Corruption in Mining – A case study

The COVID19 crisis joined the climate crisis and forced all of us as humans to reset our mindset and go back to nature. To protect it, to stop with doing business as usual, to switch towards green economy. It means to stop polluting and non-sustainable businesses first. The bigger the industry is – the bigger the pollution is and the stronger the attack to environment and climate is.

Photo 9.1 : Protest against gold mine Ilovica in Strumica- (Liljana Popovska 16.6.18)

The mining industry is one of the most polluting ones, making irreversible changes on the Earth surface and destroying biodiversity. Especially when it comes for open-pit mines, used for exploring ores of metallic mineral resources, like gold, silver, or cooper. The extraction from the ore goes with cyanide solutions or sulfuric acid, in huge pools directly in the mountain. Such improvising natural "containers" or "reactors" are like open wounds on the land, so the nature makes backlash with eco-catastrophes from time to time. There have been over 30 environmental catastrophes in mining sector in the last 25 years, reminding us that these technologies are extremely dangerous and unpredictable.

The massive incident in golden mine Baia Mare in Romania, in 2000, destroying all living beings in Danube and Tisa rivers thousands of kilometers around, was the direct reason for adopting the Mining Waste Directive (2006/21/EC) with stricter rules in protection of the environment. The practice showed that it was not enough, so the parliamentarians of the European Green Party initiated and the European Parliament adopted a Resolution on a general ban on the use of cyanide mining technologies in the European Union in May 2010.

The European Commission refused to make it obligatory, insisting that this technology is inevitable. The answer was:"The Commission is fully aware of the potential dangers linked with the use of cyanide in the mining industry... At European level, there is no ban on the use of cyanide leaching for gold extraction. According to the Treaty, Member States have the possibility to set stricter limit values." In April 2017 another European Parliament Resolution was adopted on implementation of the Mining Waste Directive (2006/21/EC). It is still up to the countries to decide how will deal with the open pit mines.

In the world, there are more than 15 localities in less than 10 countries that have already adopted regulative for complete banning of cyanide solution in golden mines in the whole country or at least at some regions that are ruined and devastated with such mining complexes. Namely, banning is valuable for the whole country in Czech Republic (2002), Costa Rica (2002), Germany (2006) and Turkey (2007), while only partly in few US states (1998-2001) and some regions in Argentina (2009).

Macedonia is too small for the big appetites of the mining business

N. Macedonia is the only country, beside Argentina, that succeeded to ban not only cyanide in open-pit golden mines, but also a sulfuric acid in open-pit cooper and other metallic mines. Was it easy? No, it was a three year extremely difficult and uncertain battle against the dangerous mines and multinacional mining corporations. It was a battle of arguments against manipulations and honesty against greed. It was a fight against two huge enemies: 1) ignorance about technology among citizens and politicians, but also 2) corruption among politicians, experts, administration and judges. The final success came as a result of civil resilience, front against mining created by local people, united with the environmentalists all over the country, Macedonian greens in the Parliament, courageous journalists, and thousands of individuals from different background.

N. Macedonia has a "fortune" to be on the road of ore rich with metallic resources, going through Balkan, namely through Romania, Serbia, Bulgaria and Greece. This is the reason why is Balkan one of the three regions, together with Caucasus and Central Asia, where the mining business for metals is focused this last decade. Another reason is probably the weak state protection of the environment, with laws that are still not implemented totally, although they are mostly done according to European directives, while some of these countries are already members of European Union. We may only speculate that the third reason for these countries to be so "popular" among mining investors is the economic situation of the countries, having a need for development, employment, and having weak state protection against corruption. Some representatives of the European banking system are playing very interesting role in such investments, supporting fake environmental studies and weak and corruptive Government officials.

The mining problem in N. Macedonia became public in 2016 with three focus points:

- The most advanced was the **open-pit cooper mine Kazandol**, which got a concession in 2015 after non-transparent procedure and approval of the Environmental Impact Assessment Study. It was in a process of building (a huge pool in the mountain, expecting new equipment) and was expected to start with work soon. This mine was built in the middle of organic plantations and next to a touristic place with a natural lake.

- The next danger was the **open-pit gold mine Ilovica**, which had a concession to start building, holding a public debate on the Environmental Impact Assessment Study. It was also planned in the middle of the agricultural valley with vegetables and fruits.

- There were over **80 locations (!!) for future mines** all over the country with concessions for examination the richness of the ores. After the examination, the concession for exploitation is expected to be given.

To understand the dimensions of the problem, we have to say that N. Macedonia is a country with a size a little smaller than Belgium, with mountains, valleys and lakes, with significant part of economy based on agriculture (cca 25% of the population), tourism and light industry. The unemployment is 16,7%, the poverty rate is 18,2% (latest available household survey data, 2017). In such atmosphere and circumstances, the corruption is expected spice.

From the environmental point of view, another visible and vivid problem is the air pollution in the big cities. It is high, due to the heavy industry from socialistic time, lousy monitoring and control, high dependence of fossil fuels in public and private sector. All this caused strong environmental movements that are fighting for clean air, against pollution of water and soil. The awareness about climate changes is raising among the wide public very fast.

So, the anti-mining movement during the last four years came on the top of the other eco-fights, making a fusion of all of them. The fight against opening mines started with the slogan of the eco-protestants: "STOP mines of death", to continue with the claim of the Macedonian green party: "Macedonia is too small for the big appetites of the mining business".

Civil resilience against opening "mines of death"

The first battles of the environmentalists were to inform and educate citizens that live near to the planned mines about the dangerous practice concerning them. Namely, such mines are destroying the nature and biodiversity, polluting water and air, as well as the water supplement itself, due to enormous quantity of water used for the pools for processing the ore. The mines, especially those with open pits, usually destroy all other economic activities in agricultural and touristic regions. After approximately 30 years work, the mines are abounded, leaving devastating surrounding, deserted area and polluted water and soil. According statistical data, the people living near such mines have bad health and numerous "mining" diseases.

Photo 9.2: Protest against the cooper mine Kazandol in Valandovo- Liljana Popovska 8.12.17

Later, the information about the so called "mines of death" (open-pit mines with cyanides and sulfuric acid) was spread out all over the country. Round tables, debates with public and on media, special "war" on social media, petitions, protests with thousands of people coming from the whole country to support local citizens. A green front was established of eco-activists from civil movement, politics and media.

In the focus of the fight were municipalities next to two mines, that were the nearest to start: Kazandol for cooper and Ilovica for gold. So, during 2017 six referendums were held with the question about opening mines on their territory. Three of them were successful, and three not, due to a strong political pressure of local authorities, defending their position with "economic growth and new jobs".

Macedonian anti-mining movement got a strong support by the green politicians from the Balkan region, but also from the top leadership of European Green Party. Their presence at the international conferences and

154

other events organized by their sister party in N. Macedonia was crucial for giving international dimension and credibility to the fight against open-pit mines. They were lobbing openly in public and with the Governmental leadership against such anachronic mining practices, proposing environmentally clean processes of gold production by recycling electronic waste. Being present always in difficult times of these battles in the period 2016-19, European Green Party showed solidarity with the green co-fighters in N. Macedonia and whole Balkan region.

Parliamentary battle for banning toxic polluters in mining

Very substantial part of the fight against opening open-pit mines of metal mineral resources was Parliamentary battle for banning toxic polluters in mining. In December 2017, a Law for mineral resources, with banning cyanide and sulfuric acid in open-pit mines was proposed by 2 Parliamentarians from the Macedonian green party DOM. The law was supported by 9 other Parliamentarians from different background and by 40 non-governmental organizations. The whole process of writing, amending, lobbing and finally adopting the Law lasted more than one year.

The Parliamentary battle itself was totally uncertain, up and down, with many surprises. It included a public broadcasted debate in the Parliament, with representatives from the mining sector, Government and civil movement. The long debate was a battlefield of different views, arguments and interests, where interested citizens could clearly see the essence of the problem. It became clear who among the parliamentarians and governmental officials have been "encouraged" to defend the undefendable positions of "mine lovers". A series of debates, interviews, gatherings and convincing on this topic followed.

Finally, in January 2019, the Law for mineral resources was adopted. Important changes were introduced: banning cyanide and sulfuric acid in new open-pit mines for metallic resources, obligatory finance guarantee for the investors in case of environmental damage, prolonged period of the procedure for getting concession for exploiting mineral resources, as well as public approach to it.

What is achieved till now

After three-years fight, the civil resilience in N. Macedonia brought significant results:

- **Open-pit cooper mine Kazandol** was closed and the Government took the concession due to breaking the Agreement for concession. Namely, the mining company was obliged to bring the equipment and be prepared to start the production within some period of time, but they have missed that. Although there were many fake reports from the mine, made by some civil servants in administration, the real state of affairs came out. The crucial proof was obtained by the State Inspector for Environment, who had finished his job professionally and made honest inspection. In fact, through the process of fighting against this mine, many speculative things connected with the procedures of approving the Environmental Impact Assessment Study and other administrative approvals and allowances in the Ministry for economy became public.

- **Open-pit gold mine Ilovica** lost his concession too, due to legal reasons. There were almost identical games with the documents, study and approvals like with the previous mine. The company is appealing now.

- **Potential 80 future mines** are under serious question, due to the newly brought Law for mineral resources. Opening new open-pit mines for metallic mineral resources with cyanide and sulfuric acid is not allowed, but also all other potential mining companies will have to deposit a proper sum as a guarantee in case of environmental damage, as well as to follow a proper procedure in front of the public.

What kind of corruptive practice faced the citizens?

Corruption is easy to detect, but not easy to proof. Without a legally proofed process, we can speak about suspicious or supposed corruptive practices in the mining sector of N. Macedonia during last decade. The proofs have to be searched in fake documents, administrative approvals, silence of the experts, hiding facts, pressure to employees and citizens, and obvious support for environmentally non-friendly practices by politicians, administrative civil servants, judges, media redactors, etc. Through all these elements, some representatives of the mining sector in the country and abroad succeeded to offer, give or solicit, directly and indirectly, something of value to influence improperly the actions of other party. We can mention few examples that look like corruption and have been debated publicly with the same arguments:

- The first steps in creating and approving mining strategy about opening over 80 mines in a small country like N. Macedonia have been done in close cooperation among mining experts and high politicians, out of the eyes of the public. Some of the mines were announced one by one later, but the citizens were not informed precisely what kind of technology was planned, so they did not react. Domestic experts were linked to foreign investors and became the most severe fighters for realization of these plans.

- The harmful mining projects were supported by the banks, which were satisfied with the formally submitted Environmental Impact Assessment Studies. They did not question their support even facing arguments contra and thousands of people been against.

- The procedure of adopting the Environmental Impact Assessment Study of the mine Kazandol was not according the law and Aarhus Convention, that means publicly announced and debated. Only hidden small meeting has been held in the municipal office. Furthermore, the content of the Study is pretty strange – although all possible damages are counted, the final conclusion is that there will not be significant changes in environment.(!) So, the expert recommended building of the mine in the middle of plantations and swimming lake, no matter that it is in very seismic zone, with high potential to pollute air, water and soil, with optional necessity to move the people living around etc.(!)

- The procedure of adopting the Environmental Impact Assessment Study of the mine Ilovica was more opened, but the content of the text was following the previous example. Although the experts were well informed and claimed openly that the mine may cause great damage to environment and people, the final conclusion was the same: recommendation for building. (!) In this case the administration of the Ministry for environment has been more cautious and did not approved the Study as a whole, but has done another strange thing – accepted some shorten version that has not been debated and published it.(!)

- The inspection of the mine Kazandol, done within the same period, was giving different results. Namely, the inspector from technical inspection "saw" that the mine equipment has been brought and installed according the Concession agreement, while another inspector for environment, came one month later and did not see anything similar. Beside two different records of inspections, there are also photos and drone-videos that proof that there was no equipment on the place. The first inspector had obviously written a record according somebody's interest.(!)

- The law for mineral resources passed two Parliamentary committee's debates and one public Parliamentary debate, after which it came on agenda at a plenary session. But, just during the reading of the title of the Law by the Parliamentary speaker, two groups of parliamentarians from two different parties (one governmental and one oppositional) run away from the plenary hall and the Law could not be voted because there was not a necessary quorum for it. (!)

- The company concessioner of the mine Ilovica appealed to the Court about the Governmental decision to cancel the concession. Although the reason for that could be easily checked and proofed, the judges decided that the company was right, without explanation. It is even more interesting that the juridical decision was brought in March 2020, during COVID19 and total lockdown, when the institutions did not work. Beside this, the Court did not publish the process and the public got the information few months later through whistling channels.(!)

There are also other numerous examples of not respecting laws, logic, dignity of the people, connected with the mining problem. But those mentioned above are enough to illustrate the matter of state and importance of honest, brave and over all, professional individuals in public sector that work according the rule of law. And the matter of state is that the citizens united in resilience front, have a power to win environmental battles and overcome corruptive individuals, whether they are politicians, administrative civil servants, judges, experts, or whoever else.

The result is changing the mindset of the citizens, but also of the politicians, who are forced by their own will or by their voters, to take a decisive steps towards fight against pollution of any kind. And corruption can be also taken as pollution. Pollution of the system.

References

Answer given by Mr. Potočnik on behalf of the Commission, European Parliament, 2010.

Assembly BILL 95, Wisconsin State Assembly, 2001.

Ban on Cyanide Mining in Montana with Initiative 137. Montana Environmental Information Center. Retrieved 28 September 2013.

Concession agreement for exploitation of gold, silver and copper in the mine "Kazandol". Ministry of Economy. Skopje. (2015).

Debate show on the topic: Real danger, or a chase against the mines? Participation of Angel Nakov from "Spas za Gevgelija", Liljana Popovska from DOM, Besa Tateshi from the Ministry of Environment, Nikolajcho Nikolov from "Buchim" and Bosko Sibinovski from "Sardic", "Kazandol". Host Ile Petrevski. TV 21. (2018).

Decision to terminate the concession agreement for exploitation of gold, silver and copper in the mine "Kazandol" with the concessionaire "Sardich MC". Government of R.S. Macedonia. Skopje. (2018).

Dimitrijevska, V. (2020). Case study for Kazandol, project "Follow the incidents - (un)intentional omissions and environmental pollution", implemented by the Association for Environmentally Sustainable Development GREEN INSTITUTE Skopje, sub-grant of the project "Together in the fight against corruption", funded by the European Union and implemented by Center for Investigative Journalism SCOOP MACEDONIA Skopje, Institute for Human Rights Skopje and Center for Community Media Development MEDIUM Gostivar.

Drone footage over the Kazandol mine. Facebook page of "Spas za Valandovo". (2017).

Environmental Impact Assessment Study of the Kazandol Mining Complex. Empiria EMC. Ministry of Environment and Physical Planning of R.S. Macedonia. Skopje. (2015).

European Parliament resolution of 27 April 2017 on implementation of the Mining Waste Directive (2006/21/EC), OJ C 298, 23.8.2018, p. 132.

European Parliament resolution of 5 May 2010 on a general ban on the use of cyanide mining technologies in the European Union, OJ C 81 E, 15.3.2011, p. 74.

Motion for a Resolution: B7-0240, European Parliament, 2010.

Rodriguez, L.G., Macias, F.A. (2009). To Cyanide or Not to Cyanide? Some Argentinean Provinces Banned Use of Cyanide in Mining Activities: Is This Prohibition Legal? Rocky Mountain Mineral Law Foundation Journal. Rocky Mountain Mineral Law Foundation. 46 (2): 237–250.

Roth, S. (2010). *Great victory against cyanide for gold mining. The Ecologist. Retrieved 25 September 2013.*

Website of the company "Sardich MC". http://www.sardich.mk.

Website of the Green Institute http://www.greeninstitute.mk/.

Јанев, А. (2018). The contract is violated, "Kazandol" can be closed. BIRN survey. Prism. Skopje.

Publications of the Green Economics Institute

The Green Economics Institute Publishing House has now published over 100 titles from leading authors and new and innovative thinkers with really new ideas and Change Making solutions for today's pressing issues! Our books are created in Open Office and many also have around 30 different writers and voices in each book, so that a variety of novel perspectives can be introduced from all around the world.

Titles available ©

Economics

Handbook of Green Economics: A Practitioner's Guide (2012) Edited By Miriam Kennet, Eleni Courea, Alan Bouquet and Ieva Pepinyte ISBN 9781907543036

Green Economics Methodology: An Introduction (2012) Edited By Tone Berg (Norway), Aase Seeberg (Norway) and Miriam Kennet ISBN 978190754357

The Green Economics Reader c (2012) Edited By Miriam Kennet ISBN 9781907543265

Rebalancing the Economy (2014) Edited by Christopher Brook, Cambridge University and Miriam Kennet. ISBN9781907543845

162

Economics of Social Justice (2015) Edited by Miriam Kennet, Iolanda Cum and Sabeeta Nathan ISBN 9781907543463

Growth for Sustainability – A Critique of Economics for the Post Oil Age (2016) Edited by Keissi Prendushi (Italy and Albania), Miriam Kennet (UK) and Federica Oriana Savarino (Sicily, Italy) ISBN 9781907543135

The Future of Income, Labour and Work (2017) Edited by Miriam Kennet. ISBN 9781907543531

Finance

The Greening of Global Finance: Reforming Global Finance c (2013) Edited By Professor Graciela Chichilnisky (USA and Argentina), Michelle S. Gale de Oliveira (USA and Brazil), Miriam Kennet, Professor Maria Madi (Brazil) and Professor Chow Fah Yee (Malaysia) ISBN 9781907543401

The Reform of Global Banking by Professor Maria Madi and Kamile Buskavaite (2015) ISBN 9781907543203

Values, Valuation and Valuing, (2017) Edited by Miriam Kennet (UK), Pamela Harling (UK), Maria Madi (Brazil and Argentina), Karen Windham Lord (Brazil and UK) ISBN 9781907543555

The Financialisation Debate (2020) Professor Maria Madi ISBN 9781913354008

The Greening of Finance, Investment and the Economy. (2021) Professor Maria Madi and Miriam Kennet ISBN 978-1-913354-24-4

Geographies of Green Economics

Greening the Global Economy (2013) Edited by Sofia Amaral (Portugal) and Miriam Kennet ISBN 9781907543944

Green Economics: The Greening of Asia and China (2012) Edited by Miriam Kennet (UK) and Norfayanti Kamaruddin (Malaysia) ISBN 9781907543234

Green Economics: Voices of Africa (2012) Edited By Miriam Kennet, Amana Winchester, Mahelet Mekonnen and Chidi Magnus Onuoha ISBN 9781907543098

The Greening of Eastern Europe (2013) Edited By Miriam Kennet and Dr Sandra Gusta (Latvia) ISBN 9781907543418

Green Economics: The Greening of Indonesia (2013) Edited By Dr Dessy Irwati and Dr Stephan Onggo (Indonesia) ISBN 9781907543821

The Greening of Latin America (2013) Edited By Michelle S. Gale de Oliveira (USA and Brazil), Maria Fernanda Caporale Madi (Brazil), Carlos Francisco Restituyo Vassallo (Dominican Republic) and Miriam Kennet ISBN 9781907543876

Africa: Transition to a Green Economy (2013) Edited By Dr Chidi Magnus (Nigeria) ISBN 9781907543364

Green Economics & India (2014) Edited by Professor Natalie West, Professor Indira Dutta, Odeta Grabauskaitė, Kanupriya Bhagat and Miriam Kennet ISBN 9781907543500

The Greening of the Mediterranean Economy (2013) Edited by Miriam Kennet, Dr Michael Briguglio, Dr Enrico Tezza, Michelle S Gale de Oliveira and Doaa Salman ISBN 9781907543906

The European Economy: Crisis and Recovery (2014) Edited by Miriam Kennet ISBN 9781907543463

The Eastern European Economy, Policy and Practise for Recovery, (July 2014) Professor Dr Dzintra Astaja (Latvia) and Odeta Grabauskaitė (Lithuania) ISBN 9781907543890

The Greening of Italy: Crisis and Recovery (2014) Edited by Alberto Truccolo ISBN 9781097543920

Landfill in Latvia: Scientific Monograph- Towards a circular economy (2020) Professor Natālija Cudečka-Purina & Dzintra Atstāja ISBN 978-1-913354-03-9

The Greening of Japan (2021) Koryo Suzuki ISBN 978-1-913354-15-2

Health and Well Being

The Greening of Health and Well Being (2012) Edited by Katherine Kennet, Michelle Gale de Oliveira and Miriam Kennet ISBN 9781907543760

NHS Continuing Health Care (2016) Edited by Peter Lang (UK) ISBN 9781907543753

Survival Solutions: Economy, Biodiversity, Health and Climate (2021) edited by Sukriti Anand ISBN 978-1-913354-04-6

Social Policy

The Greening of Health and Well being (2013) Edited By Michelle S. Gale de Oliveira, Miriam Kennet and Dr Katherine Kennet ISBN 9781907543760

The Vintage Generation, the Rocking Chair Revolution (2015) Edited by Miriam Kennet and Birgit Meinhard – Schiebel (Austria) ISBN 9781907543517

Citizen's Income and Green Economics (2012) By Clive Lord, edited by Judith Felton and Miriam Kennet ISBN 9781907543074

Green Economics: Women's Unequal Pay and Poverty (2012) Edited By Miriam Kennet, Michelle S Gale de Oliveira, Judith Felton and Amana Winchester ISBN 9781907543081

Young People: Green Jobs, Employment and Education (2012) Edited By Miriam Kennet and Juliane Goeke (Germany) ISBN 9781907543258

The Philosophy of Social Justice (2015) Edited by Miriam Kennet and Samuel Gilmore ISBN 9781907543739

Fairtrade (2016) Jessica Bosseaux ISBN 9781907543708

Energy and Climate Policy

Green Economics and Climate Change (2012) Edited By Miriam Kennet and Winston Ka-Ming Mak (Hong Kong and UK)

Green Economics: The Greening of Energy Policies (2012) Edited By Ryota Koike (Japan) and Miriam Kennet ISBN 9781907543326

Rolling back the tide of climate change: energy policy in the USA and China (2015) Professor Peter Yang Autumn 2015 ISBN 9781907543777

Renewables are getting cheaper (2016) Edited by Professor Peter Yang ISBN 9781907543722

Biomassa Algale (Autumn 2015) Iolanda Cum. (Italy) ISBN 9781907543982

Renewable Energy Economics in Egypt and the MENA Region (2016) by Hend Ahmed Mohamed Mohamed Saadeldin Edited by Francesca Galli (2016) ISBN 9781907543173

Renewable Energy Choices: Stories from the Transition to renewables. (2016) Jasmeet Phagoora, Federica Savarino,(Italy) Miriam Kennet and Iolanda Cum (Italy) ISBN 9781907543166

Climate Justice (2021) Irene Garcia. ISBN 978-1-913354-05-3

Climate Change: The Inner Landscapes. (2021) Jeremy Seabrook. ISBN 978-1-913354-08-4

Food, Farming and Agriculture

Green Economics & Food, Farming and Agriculture (2013) Edited by Michelle S. Gale de Oliveira, Rose Blackett-Ord and Miriam Kennet ISBN 9781907543449

Greening the food on your plate (2013) Edited by Michelle S. Gale de Oliveira, Rose Blackett-Ord and Miriam Kennet ISBN 9781907543654

Biodiversity, conservation and animal protection

Biodiversity Loss: The Variety of Life Under Threat (2015) Anna Wainer, Odeta Grabauskaitė and Miriam Kennet ISBN 9781907543227

Endangered Ecosystems. (2021) Jay Beeks, Alexander Ziko, Nicole Cox and Sukhmani SingaISBN 978-1-913354-07-7

Lifestyle

The Green Transport Revolution (2013) Edited By Richard Holcroft and Miriam Kennet ISBN 9781907543968

Green Poetry, Art and Photography (2013) Edited by Dr Matt Rinaldi, Rose Blackett-Ord, Friedericke Oeser Prasse and Miriam Kennet ISBN 9781907543784

The Green Built Environment: A Handbook (2012) Edited By Miriam Kennet and Judith Felton ISBN 9781907543067

Building Sustainable Communities: Life and Thoughts of Henry Cox (2016) Edited by Henry Fieglar ISBN 9781907543197

Landfill in Latvia. Towards a Circular Economy (2021) Natālija Cudečka-Purina & Dzintra Atstāja ISBN 978-1-913354-03-9

Philosophy

Integrating Ethics, Social Responsibility and Governance, (2013) Edited by Tore Audin Hedin, (Norway), Michelle Gale de Oliveira, Miriam Kennet ISBN 9781907543395

The Philosophical Basis of the Green Movement (2013) Edited by Professor Michael Benfield, Miriam Kennet and Michelle Gale de Oliveira (Brazil) ISBN 9781907543548

Green Culture, Cultures and Philosophy (2016) Edited by Nelly Eysholdt and Miriam Kennet ISBN9781907543661

The future as a vision: From the Anthropocene to the Biocene. (2021) Professor Maria Madi and Miriam Kennet. ISBN 978-1-913354-01-5

Migration

Introducing Migration (2016) Edited by Henry Fieglar and Miriam Kennet ISBN 9781907543210

Stewardship Economy Series

Stewardship Economy (2021) by Julian Pratt. Book 1 ISBN 978-1-913354-09-1

Stewardship Economy: How to make it work. Book 2 (2021) by Julian Pratt ISBN 978-1-913354-11-4

Printed by Printforce, United Kingdom